THE ULTIMATE RETIREMENT PLANNING BLUEPRINT

THE SIMPLE 6 STEP FORMULA

PINPOINT YOUR RETIREMENT VISION, CALCULATE SAVINGS GOALS AND RETIRE WITH FINANCIAL FREEDOM

PIERCE SULLIVAN

CONTENTS

'I can't afford it' shuts down your brain. 'How can I afford it?' open up possibilities, excitement and dreams.

ROBERT KIYOSAKI

INTRODUCTION: THE LATE BLOOM

The dream of a comfortable retirement - once considered a natural progression of the American life cycle - has become increasingly complex over the past decade. As I wrote this book in 2024, I reflected on the dramatic shifts that have reshaped how we think about, plan for, and approach our retirement years.

The 2010s and early 2020s brought unprecedented challenges to retirement planning. We witnessed historically low interest rates that diminished traditional savings vehicles, a global pandemic that disrupted careers and depleted emergency funds, and rising housing costs that forced many to choose between current needs and future security. The explosion of the gig economy has meant that millions of workers now navigate retirement planning without the traditional support of employer-sponsored 401(k)s. Meanwhile, rising healthcare costs have cast a long shadow over retirement calculations, with the average couple now needing to set aside hundreds of thousands of dollars for medical expenses alone.

Yet within these challenges lie opportunities. The accessibility and democratization of investment tools has made sophisticated retirement planning accessible to more people than ever before. Digital platforms have simplified portfolio management, while the rise of target-date funds and robo-advisors has brought professional-grade investment strategies to everyday savers. The remote work revolution has opened new possibilities for phased retirement, allowing many to extend their earning years on their own terms.

This book arrives at a crucial moment. Recent surveys show that nearly 64% of Americans are behind on their retirement savings, with millennials and Gen X expressing particular concern about their financial futures. But rather than view this as a crisis, I see it as a call to action. Whether you're just starting your career, approaching your peak earning years, or within sight of retirement, there has never been a better time to take control of your financial destiny.

In the following chapters, we'll explore practical strategies for building retirement security in today's dynamic environment. We'll examine how to leverage new opportunities while protecting against modern risks. Most importantly, we'll create a roadmap that works with your unique circumstances and goals.

The path to a secure retirement may look different than it did for previous generations, but it remains achievable. With the right knowledge, tools, and mindset, you can build the retirement you envision - no matter where you're starting from. Let's begin that journey together.

This book serves as your roadmap to navigating the modern landscape of retirement planning. We have designed it to simplify this often overwhelming process. You will learn in six key stages how to build a secure and satisfying future.

We start with understanding your current financial situation. Then, we move on to setting goals and creating a budget. We will explore savings, investment options, healthcare, and estate planning. Each chapter builds on the last, creating a complete picture of your retirement plan. We help you tackle topics like taxes, estate planning, Medicare, and budgeting step by step. However, most importantly, our approach is holistic. We don't just focus on numbers. We consider your life, health, and dreams. Retirement is not just about money. It's about enjoying the freedom to do what you love. Our goal is to make sure you can live comfortably and confidently.

This book is not just words on a page. It is interactive. You'll find activities and planning tools designed to help you apply what you learn. You will have the chance to reflect, develop, and act. These tools are designed to make your journey more engaging and productive.

I invite you to take action. The art of planning tomorrow is as individual as you are. Your canvas is shaped by life's realities: family needs, career choices, health considerations, and personal dreams.

Just as no two artists create identical works, no two retirement journeys follow the same path. The tools you choose—whether 401(k)s, IRAs, real estate investments, or passion projects—are like different brushes in your kit. Some prefer the structure of traditional retirement accounts, while others prefer alternative investments' flexibility. Each choice adds texture and depth to your financial composition. This isn't about following a predetermined pattern—it's about crafting a future that reflects your personal vision, values, and dreams. With each page, you will gain more understanding and confidence.

The data is precise. As a society, we are experiencing a monumental shift in our retirement readiness. The landscape has never been so varied, with significant differences across generations and genders. Men are almost a third more likely to be confident about their retirement futures than women. Additionally, 70% of women need clarification about translating savings into monthly income. This has massive repercussions for our communities and poses a considerable risk that we outlive our savings.

According to the findings, today's retirees are increasingly drawn to dependable income sources and proactive investment oversight. The clear differences between demographic categories suggest where targeted financial education could help bridge preparation gaps. It's time we all had access to knowledge and know-how that we can both understand and apply.

The Holistic Principles and Steps in this book apply to anyone, any country, any age. However, you will notice some of the specific Tax references relate to US tax laws and policies. We advise you to seek local tax and financial counsel in your area if this is not applicable to you.

We want you to feel optimistic and excited about the years ahead. Retirement is not an end. It is a new beginning filled with opportunities.

Together, let's turn overwhelming into manageable. Let's turn uncertainty into clarity. Let's ensure your retirement years are some of the best years of your life.

Welcome to your new journey. Be Retirement Ready.

CHAPTER 1
LAYING THE FOUNDATION FOR YOUR GOLDEN YEARS

For those who retired in the 1970s, their pension plans promised a steady income for life. Fast forward to today, and most retirees no longer have such guarantees. The landscape of Retirement has shifted significantly over the decades. The days of a "golden handshake" and a secure pension are long gone for many. We now face a world where individuals must independently navigate the complexities of retirement planning.

Based on surveys and research, we know people's biggest concerns about retirement are:

1. Running Out of Money
    - Fear of outliving savings
    - Impact of inflation on purchasing power
    - Unexpected medical expenses
    - Long-term care costs
2. Healthcare Costs
    - Medicare coverage gaps
    - Rising medical costs
    - Prescription drug expenses

    - Long-term care insurance needs
3. Social Security Uncertainty
    - Future benefit availability
    - Adequacy of benefits
    - Best age to start claiming
    - Program's long-term sustainability
4. Market Volatility
    - Investment risk in retirement
    - Sequence of returns risk
    - Portfolio sustainability
    - Market crashes affecting savings
5. Timing Issues
    - Determining the right age to retire
    - Estimating the right amount of saving
    - Playing catch-up on retirement savings
    - Forced early retirement due to health/job loss
6. Lifestyle Concerns
    - Maintaining current standard of living
    - Housing decisions (downsizing, aging in place)
    - Supporting adult children/grandchildren
    - Having enough for travel/hobbies
7. Care Dependencies
    - Becoming a burden on family
    - Affording assisted living
    - Quality of care options
    - Maintaining independence

This chapter will guide you through understanding the changes in the retirement landscape and lay the foundations for your retirement plan.

1.1 UNDERSTANDING THE RETIREMENT LANDSCAPE

You deserve to feel safe about your future after a lifetime of hard work.

Major events of the past few years—including the pandemic, ongoing market volatility, and rising inflation—have left many people feeling stressed about their financial futures.

This challenging period magnifies the cracks in our retirement system. Half of private-sector workers need access to a workplace retirement plan, and nearly half of all adults aged 55 to 65 have no personal retirement savings.

We are living longer.

Americans now live about 30 years longer than they did in 1900. This is a double-edged sword. On the one hand, it means more time to enjoy life after work. On the other, it requires more savings to sustain a longer retirement. Planning must consider how to save and how to make those savings last. The challenge is to balance enjoying the present with preparing for the future. Many people need to pay more attention to how long they will live and how much they will need.

Today's retired couples need to set aside roughly $300,000 to cover basic medical expenses during Retirement - and that figure doesn't include the growing concern about cognitive care costs. With Alzheimer's cases expected to double to 12.7 million Americans by 2050, the financial burden of healthcare in Retirement is becoming even more daunting.

The Rise of 401(K)

Retirement planning has evolved dramatically over the last century. In the early days, defined benefit plans were standard. These plans promised a fixed payout upon Retirement. Your employer, not you, managed the investment risk. This changed with the introduction of defined contribution plans like the 401(k) in the late 20th century. Here, the responsibility shifted to you, the employee. You decide how much to contribute and how to invest it. This shift has increased the importance of personal financial literacy. You must now actively engage with your retirement savings to ensure they meet your future needs.

As a society we are living longer , but we are also facing higher healthcare costs, and have lost one of our most reliable sources of guaranteed lifetime income. It's a perfect storm of increasing expenses and decreasing financial security.

Diverse Retirement Experiences

Many retirees continue to work part-time or engage in "gig" work. This trend allows them to supplement their income and stay active. Technology has also impacted retirement planning. Online tools and apps make it easier to track savings and investments. They offer new ways to manage your finances but require you to stay informed and cautious about digital security. Understanding these tools can empower you to take control of your financial future.

Retirement experiences are as diverse as the people planning them. Cultural differences play a role in how Retirement is perceived and approached. In some cultures, family plays a significant role. In others, independence is valued more highly. The age at which people retire and their chosen lifestyle can vary widely.

This diversity means there is no one-size-fits-all solution. Your retirement plan should reflect your values and circumstances.

Government policies also influence retirement planning. Social security remains a cornerstone for many retirees. However, its future is uncertain. Changes in tax laws can affect how much you save and how you withdraw funds in Retirement. Staying informed about these changes is crucial. They can have significant impacts on your financial planning. You must adapt your strategies to align with new laws and regulations. Policies can change, but you can navigate these shifts effectively with the proper knowledge.

1.2 THE SIX STEP FORMULA

This guide is structured around six pivotal steps, complemented by an array of Tools and Workbooks crafted to simplify your retirement planning process. Initiating this journey might seem overwhelming, but our resources are tailored for ease of use, guiding you smoothly towards your goals. By reaching this point, you've already accomplished a significant milestone. Together, we will delve into each step, empowering you to create a personalized Blueprint.

Step 1 - Defining Your Retirement Vision and Goals

Step 2 - Understanding The Control Equation

Step 3 - Retire On Your Own Terms; Know Your Sources of Income, Claims and Costs

Step 4 - Your Blueprint: The Spending vs. Savings Juggle

Step 5 - Investment Planning

Step 6 - Holistic Retirement Considerations - Are you Ready?

1.3 COMMON RETIREMENT PITFALLS AND HOW TO AVOID THEM

In Retirement, financial pitfalls can be as treacherous as any obstacle. One common mistake is inadequate savings. This can lead to overspending in the early years of Retirement. Imagine withdrawing large sums from your savings, only to find yourself short later. This can cause stress and financial strain. Another error is the mismanagement of retirement accounts. Some people need to review their investment strategies more. They may not adjust them to suit their new life stage. They might leave funds in high-risk investments, which can lead to losses. This is especially risky as you age and have less time to recover from market downturns.

Beyond finances, retirees face lifestyle pitfalls that can impact their well-being. Social isolation is a significant concern. Many people find their social circles shrinking after leaving work. Without the daily interaction of a job, loneliness can set in. This can affect mental health. It can also reduce life satisfaction. Neglecting health is another pitfall. Without the routine of a job, some retirees become less active. They might skip regular exercise or eat poorly. This can lead to health problems. These problems can reduce quality of life and increase medical costs.

Transitioning into retirement can either be overwhelming or feel quite natural. It's a deeply personal experience, often accompanied by financial concerns and lifestyle changes. The shift from a structured work life to having ample free time can lead to uncertainty and anxiety. Adjusting to a fixed income and the worry of depleting savings are common stressors. Additionally, the absence of daily work routines might make it challenging to find purpose and direction. Recognizing and understanding these changes are crucial steps in managing the transition into retirement smoothly.

Flexibility in planning is critical. Life is unpredictable, and unexpected events can disrupt even the best-laid plans. Develop a contingency plan. This helps you adapt to changes without derailing your Retirement. Consider setting aside an emergency fund. This fund can cover unforeseen expenses. Revisit your retirement plan regularly. Adjust it as needed based on your circumstances. This ensures you remain on track to meet your goals.

Proactive planning is key to avoiding these pitfalls. It requires awareness and action. By understanding and planning for these challenges, you can enjoy a more secure and rewarding retirement.

Each of the SIX STEPS we outline will cover proactive planning and how to avoid pitfalls.

1.4 THE IMPORTANCE OF HOLISTIC RETIREMENT PLANNING

Holistic retirement planning considers every part of your life, not just money. This approach looks at your health, emotional well-being, and social life. It makes sure all these parts work together for a happy retirement. When you plan this way, you think about how each part of your life affects the others. For example, having enough money can reduce stress. Less stress can lead to better mental health. Feeling good mentally, you might be more active and engaged in your community. Being socially active can improve your physical health. So, all these parts are connected. When planning for Retirement, you cannot look at just one part of your life.

Financial security is essential, but it's not the only thing. Feeling safe about your finances can help you feel better mentally. When you know you have enough money for the future, you can relax. This allows you to enjoy life more. You will have less worry about unexpected expenses. This peace of mind is vital for good mental health. When you feel mentally sound, you are more likely to take care of your physical health. You might exercise more and eat better. This creates a positive cycle where each part of your life supports the others.

Social engagement plays a significant role in your physical health. Staying connected with friends and family keeps you active. Joining clubs or groups can give you a sense of purpose. This can lead to a healthier lifestyle. Studies show that people who stay socially active live longer. They also report better health. This is because social activities can motivate you to stay physically active. They also provide support during tough times. Feeling part of a community makes you less likely to feel lonely. This can help prevent health problems linked to social isolation.

Continuous planning is key to a holistic approach. Life changes, and your plans should, too. Regularly check your retirement goals and make adjustments if needed. This helps you stay on track. Your needs and desires might change over time. You might want to travel more or focus on hobbies. Your health might change, requiring more care or different activities. By revisiting your plans, you can adapt to these changes. This keeps your Retirement aligned with your current life.

To help you with holistic planning, we provide tools like checklists in Step 5. These tools make sure you consider all parts of your life.

Holistic planning is about seeing the big picture and ensuring all parts of your life work together. This way, you can have a financially secure and fulfilling retirement. You want a retirement where you can enjoy your time, stay healthy, and feel connected to others. You can truly enjoy your golden years when all these parts come together.

1.5 THE RETIREMENT TAPESTRY - WHERE DO YOU FIT?

Are you Retirement Ready? Take our Quiz

Every individual's situation carries its nuances and complexities. Yet, often, we are closer to being prepared for Retirement than we realize. This quiz serves as a realistic checkpoint, helping you understand your current standing and highlighting areas to focus on.

The Readiness Score doesn't quantify your current income or savings—details we can't access—nor does it serve as an official assessment of your personal circumstances. Instead, it offers a glimpse into your retirement preparedness, grounded in typical behaviours and history, to gauge your Retirement Readiness

Interactive Exercise: Retirement Readiness Assessment

Part 1: Assessment Quiz

Rate each statement on a scale of 1-5:

1 = Strongly Disagree

2 = Disagree

3 = Neutral

4 = Agree

5 = Strongly Agree

Financial Knowledge

- I understand how compound interest works
- I can explain the difference between stocks and bonds
- I know my current tax bracket and how retirement savings affect my taxes
- I understand how inflation impacts retirement savings
- I'm familiar with different retirement account types (401(k), IRA, etc.)

Savings Behavior

- I consistently save money each month
- I automatically contribute to retirement accounts
- I take advantage of any employer matching for retirement contributions
- I increase my savings rate when I receive a raise
- I track my spending and maintain a budget

Debt Management

- I have no credit card debt
- My total monthly debt payments are less than 36% of my gross income
- I have a plan to be debt-free (except mortgage) by retirement
- I avoid taking on new debt for depreciating assets
- I understand the terms and interest rates of all my debts

Age & Timing Planning

- I have calculated how much money I'll need in retirement
- I have a target retirement age in mind

- My investment mix is appropriate for my age
- I have considered healthcare costs in my retirement planning
- I regularly review and adjust my retirement strategy

Part 2: Scoring Guide

Calculate separate scores for each category:

- Financial Knowledge: Questions 1-5
- Savings Behavior: Questions 6-10
- Debt Management: Questions 11-15
- Age & Timeline Planning: Questions 16-20

Part 3: Map Your Score on the Financial Readiness Matrix

Now its time to add together your scores

Step 1

Add the total of your score /25 from "Financial Knowledge" plus your score /25 from "Age & Timing Planning". This will give you a TOTAL /50.

The addition of these 2 elements is called your FOUNDATION KNOWLEDGE SCORE. This is shown on the Horizontal Axis on the chart below.

Step 2

Add the total of your score /25 from "Savings Behaviour" plus your score /25 from "Debt Management". This will give you a TOTAL /50.

The addition of these 2 elements is called your PREPARATION SCORE. This is shown on the Vertical Axis on the chart below.

Step 3

The intersection of these two scores on the matrix will give you an indication of how Retirement Ready you are. Have a go and see where you land.

Financial Readiness Matrix

Part 4 - What Does This Mean?

Whatever your profile, remember that knowledge is exciting.

The labels in this matrix are intended to give you a "moment in time" snapshot. You are not stuck in this place and it is not "good" or "bad". It is simply a way for you to take an honest snapshot of what stage you are at in planning for your future.

The tools and information contained in the rest of this book will put you in the perfect position to build knowledge, take action and alleviate procrastination. There is always an opportunity to shift through this matrix to improve your Confidence and Readiness. Your journey starts now.

CHAPTER 2
STEP 1: DEFINING YOUR RETIREMENT VISION AND GOALS

"The goal isn't more money. The goal is living life on your own terms."

CHRIS BROGAN

2.1 KNOW WHERE YOU ARE HEADED

Retirement is a significant transition that can bring stress. But with the right strategies, you can manage this stress effectively. Setting new personal goals is essential for a fulfilling retirement. Goals provide direction and motivation, helping you focus your energy on meaningful pursuits.

Imagine stepping into a life where every day promises new experiences and opportunities. This is the essence of creating a vivid retirement vision. Visualizing your ideal retirement involves imagining the lifestyle you wish to lead. For some, it might be a cozy home by a lake, waking up to the gentle sounds of water. Others may dream of travelling the world, exploring new cultures, and tasting exotic foods. Consider where you see yourself living. Do you picture a bustling city with endless activities or a quiet countryside with peace and tranquility? These dreams form the Blueprint for your Retirement.

Setting specific and achievable goals is crucial. Goals act as a roadmap to guide your decisions and actions. Aim to set financial independence milestones. These could include paying off your mortgage or building a nest egg that will last your lifetime. Personal growth and learning objectives also play a role. You may want to learn a new language or take up a hobby you've always wanted. Goals give you direction and purpose. They help you measure your progress and keep you motivated.

Retirement is not just a financial shift but a significant emotional and psychological transition. Many people struggle with the loss of work identity. Your career may have defined you for decades. Without it, you might feel adrift. Developing coping strategies is essential. Stay active and engaged in activities that bring joy and satisfaction. Volunteering, joining clubs, or starting new projects can help fill the gap left by work. Emotional preparation helps you embrace this new phase with a positive outlook.

Creating a holistic retirement vision and setting measurable goals requires thoughtful reflection. Take the time to consider what you truly want. Think about what will bring you happiness and fulfilment. Remember, your retirement is your time to live life on your terms.

Interactive Exercise: Self-Reflection and Purpose Discovery

Take some time for self-reflection. Consider these journaling prompts to uncover your values and desires:

Financial & Lifestyle

1. What does an ideal day in retirement look like to me, from morning to evening?
2. How do I define "purpose" and "fulfilment" at this stage of my life?
3. What activities or hobbies have I always wanted to pursue but never had time for?
4. How much structure vs. flexibility do I want in my daily routine?
5. What role do I want work to play in my life, if any? (consulting, part-time, volunteering)

Health & Wellbeing

6. What habits or practices do I want to develop to maintain my physical and mental health?
7. How can I create and maintain meaningful social connections outside of work?
8. What brings me joy and energy, and how can I incorporate more of it into my life?
9. How do I want to challenge myself intellectually?

Relationships & Legacy

10. How do I envision my role in my family evolving? (as a parent, grandparent, spouse)

11. What knowledge, skills, or values do I want to pass on to others?
12. How do I want to contribute to my community?
13. What mark do I want to leave on the world?

Location & Environment

14. Where do I want to live? Is my current location ideal for my retirement vision?
15. What kind of living arrangement would best support my desired lifestyle?
16. How important is proximity to family, healthcare, cultural activities, or nature?

Personal Growth

17. What parts of myself have I neglected that I'd like to develop?
18. What fears or limiting beliefs do I need to address about this life transition?
19. What would make me feel proud when I look back on my retirement years?
20. What new skills or areas of knowledge would I like to develop?

As you answer these questions, patterns may emerge. These insights can guide you in setting goals and choosing activities that resonate with your true self. Reflecting on these questions helps clarify your vision for Retirement, making it more intentional and satisfying.

Retirement is a significant life transition that can unsettle even the most prepared individuals. The key is to remain open to change.

Transitioning into retirement can be made smoother by shifting to part-time work or consulting roles, easing financial pressures while keeping you mentally and socially active. This approach not only maintains a sense of purpose but also facilitates the establishment of a new routine. Incorporating regular exercise, hobbies, and social activities into your schedule can help fill your days with meaning, offering stability and reducing stress.

Consulting financial advisors and retirement coaches can greatly improve your retirement vision. Their expert advice helps you make informed decisions, customize plans to fit your needs, and simplify the complexities of retirement. They play a crucial role in enhancing investments, defining realistic goals, and keeping you motivated. Additionally, using interactive tools like roadmap templates and scenario planning exercises makes planning more engaging. These resources help you set clear goals, anticipate challenges, and adopt a forward-thinking mindset. This combination of professional guidance and practical planning tools steers you away from common pitfalls, empowering you to confidently manage your retirement journey.

Your roadmap is not a one-time task. It's essential to revisit and revise it regularly. Life changes and your plan should change with it. Set regular intervals to review your plan. This could be every six months or once a year. Assess your progress and make adjustments as needed. Your priorities have shifted. Your financial situation has changed. Keeping your plan up-to-date ensures it remains relevant and practical. It helps you remain flexible and adaptable. This ongoing evaluation keeps your retirement goals aligned with your current life.

Building a personalized retirement roadmap takes effort. It requires you to think deeply about your future. It asks you to consider your current situation and future needs. It challenges you to define your values and priorities. It encourages you to seek professional advice and engage in interactive planning.

Most importantly, it asks you to commit to ongoing evaluation. This process helps you build a retirement that is both secure and fulfilling. It gives you confidence and peace of mind. With a clear roadmap, you can look forward to the future and embrace the opportunities that Retirement will bring.

Your Retirement Vision Board

A vision board is a collection of images and words that represent your goals, priorities, values and dreams. It is a simple yet powerful tool to transform abstract thinking into tangible goals. This vision board acts as a constant reminder to stay focused and driven. Neuroscientist Dr Tara Swart sheds light on the science behind this: "Viewing images on a vision board activates the brain to recognise opportunities that might otherwise be overlooked". The brain performs a process known as 'value-tagging,' embedding significant items into your subconscious, thereby sifting through and ignoring the irrelevant."

Your Vision Board is a visual summary of everything that matters most to you. Reflect on the answers to your questions in the previous Task "Self Reflection and Purpose Discovery": Revisit what brings you joy,security and fulfilment.

Start by gathering materials like magazines, scissors, and glue. You can also opt for a digital board using tools like Pinterest or Canva. Collect pictures, phrases, and quotes that resonate with the themes in your "Self Reflection and Purpose Discovery". Arrange them on a large piece of paper or digitally, piecing them together like a puzzle. Each image should evoke a sense of purpose and possibility.

The process of creating a vision board goes beyond just assembling pictures. It involves a profound reflection on your values and goals. As you choose each image, ask yourself why it speaks to you. Does it represent a long-held dream or a new ambition? This reflection aligns your daily actions with your broader aspirations. Once your board is complete, place it somewhere you see every day. This constant visual cue reinforces your commitment to your goals. It reminds you of the life you are working toward, motivating you to take steps.

As you embark on this creative process, remember the endless possibilities.

2.2 BUILDING A SPECIFIC, PERSONALIZED ACTION PLAN

Having a personalized action plan creates clarity and a sense of security. It gives us a tailored strategy that aligns your daily actions with your retirement goals.

Such a plan gives structure to your Self Discovery and to your Vision Board, turning both these explorative tools into achievable steps. It acts as a guide, helping you make decisions that support your goals and fit within your timelines. Crafting this plan involves setting clear objectives, both short-term and long-term. Short-term goals include adjusting your budget or exploring new hobbies. Long-term goals involve ensuring financial stability or planning a move to a new location. By defining these targets, you can prioritize your actions based on what's most urgent and impactful, ensuring you spend time and resources on what matters most.

To create your action plan, start by pinpointing your objectives. Consider what you aim to achieve soon and in the long run. Break these goals into smaller, achievable tasks. For instance, if your goal is to travel, start by researching destinations or saving money for your travel fund.

Tracking your progress is crucial for staying on course. Use tools that suit your style, whether a digital app or a traditional planner. They help maintain focus and accountability. These resources can also help you adjust your plan as needed. Life can be unpredictable, and having the flexibility to adapt ensures your plan remains relevant. Regularly review your action plan, checking off completed tasks and updating priorities as circumstances change. This ongoing process keeps your momentum, allowing you to celebrate small victories. It also helps identify areas where you might need to adjust your strategy, ensuring your plan continues aligning with your vision.

To illustrate the power of a personalized action plan, consider the story of a retiree who wanted to transition gradually into leisure activities. Their plan included short-term goals like reducing work hours and joining local clubs. Long-term, they aimed to spend winters in a warmer climate. By prioritizing these actions, they managed the shift smoothly, maintaining a fulfilling lifestyle while easing into Retirement. Another individual focused their plan on achieving financial milestones. They set objectives to pay off outstanding debts and increase their savings. By tracking their progress, they could see their financial health improve, giving them the confidence to retire with peace of mind.

Creating a personalized action plan is about more than just organizing tasks. It's about aligning your daily efforts with your overarching goals. This plan becomes a living document, evolving as your needs and circumstances change. It provides clarity and direction, helping you make informed decisions that support your retirement vision.

Interactive Exercise: Action Plan

What you will need in front of you:

1. Your Answers from Interactive Exercise: "Self Reflection and Purpose Discovery"
2. Your Vision Board

We now ask you to refine your answers and images from the above exercises into a set of short and long term objectives. Please take your time. Ensure you develop THREE different objectives for each important area in your life

- 1 Year Objective
- 5 Year Objective
- 10 Year Objective

Don't worry if it seems far away and difficult to imagine right now. Just start! It's perfectly acceptable to have an extensive list of Desires and Self-Reflections, while keeping your Specific Objectives more concise. This approach streamlines your Actions, making them more achievable in smaller, manageable steps. The more you engage in establishing PACT goals—objectives that are Purposeful/Meaningful to your long-term aspirations, Actionable with outcomes within your control, Continuous, allowing for repetition over time, and Trackable—the process will become simpler and more intuitive.

As a reminder, the Key Areas to develop your objectives are

- Financial & Lifestyle
- Health & Well-being
- Relationships & Legacy

- Location & Environment
- Personal Growth

Enjoy the Process. Have fun with it. Get Ready to feel inspired.

2.3 MONTHLY REFLECTION AND REVIEW

Reflecting keeps us in check and challenges us to see if our Actions align with our Vision. It is easy for Action Plans to become stale and one-dimensional. The act of regular reflection keeps us honest and ensures we feel optimistic and motivated to stick to the plan we have developed.

Set aside time once a month to write or reflect on your core beliefs.

There may be discrepancies between what you value and how you spend your time or resources. Identifying these gaps can be enlightening. Perhaps you value family but spend little time with loved ones, or the plan you have developed doesn't allow you to spend time with your loved ones. Or you might prioritize health but neglect regular exercise. Recognizing these inconsistencies is the first step to realignment. It allows you to adjust your actions to ensure they mirror your values.

One Month after you have set your Initial Action Plan, we advise you to revisit your Goals. The reason we advise you to do this one month later is that you will have many elements to overcome, reassess, clarify, and crystalize as you start this process. Usually, it takes time for us to better understand what we actually need and want from this process. Life changes and your priorities may shift over time. Being open to these changes and adjusting your goals accordingly keeps them relevant. Peer group discussions can also provide support. Sharing insights with others facing similar transitions can offer new perspectives. These discussions reinforce your commitment to value-driven goals, providing encouragement and accountability.

As this chapter closes, remember that tracking and adjusting your plans is not a one-time task. It's a continuous process that supports your retirement journey. Stay proactive in monitoring your progress. Be willing to adapt when life throws you a curveball. This approach keeps you in control, allowing you to enjoy your Retirement to the fullest. In the following chapter, we will explore how to embrace a fulfilling retirement, focusing on activities that bring joy and purpose to your days.

CHAPTER 3
STEP 2: UNDERSTANDING THE CONTROL EQUATION

"Do what you can, with what you have, where you are."

THEODORE ROOSEVELT

3.1 THE RETIREMENT CONTROL EQUATION

Navigating the journey to retirement is multi-faceted, with some aspects beyond our grasp, like fluctuating markets and changes in laws. However, we hold power over critical elements, such as enhancing our health to extend our working years and life and deciding when to retire. To carve a path to a comfortable retirement, it's crucial to concentrate on what we can influence. This principle is often called the 'control equation' - focusing our energy and resources on variables within our control while acknowledging and planning around those we cannot.

Within our control are key decisions like our savings rate, lifestyle choices, skill development, and investment costs. We can choose to live below our means, consistently save a portion of our income, and regularly update our professional skills to maintain earning potential. We can also control our investment expenses by selecting low-cost funds and minimizing transaction fees. Perhaps most importantly, we can safeguard our health through regular exercise, proper nutrition, and preventive healthcare - investments that can significantly impact both our earning capacity and retirement quality.

Outside our control are market returns, inflation rates, future tax policies, and global economic conditions. While we can't direct these factors, we can build resilience against them through diversification, maintaining emergency funds, and creating multiple income streams. The control equation suggests that rather than worrying about these uncontrollable elements, we should focus on optimizing our controllable variables to create a robust retirement strategy that can weather various scenarios.

Understanding and applying the control equation helps transform retirement planning from an overwhelming challenge into a series of manageable decisions and actions. By directing our attention and efforts toward what we can influence, we create a more empowering and effective approach to retirement preparation."

The following diagram helps show that while some critical retirement factors are outside your control, you can still significantly impact your retirement outcomes through the decisions you make in areas where you have full or partial control.

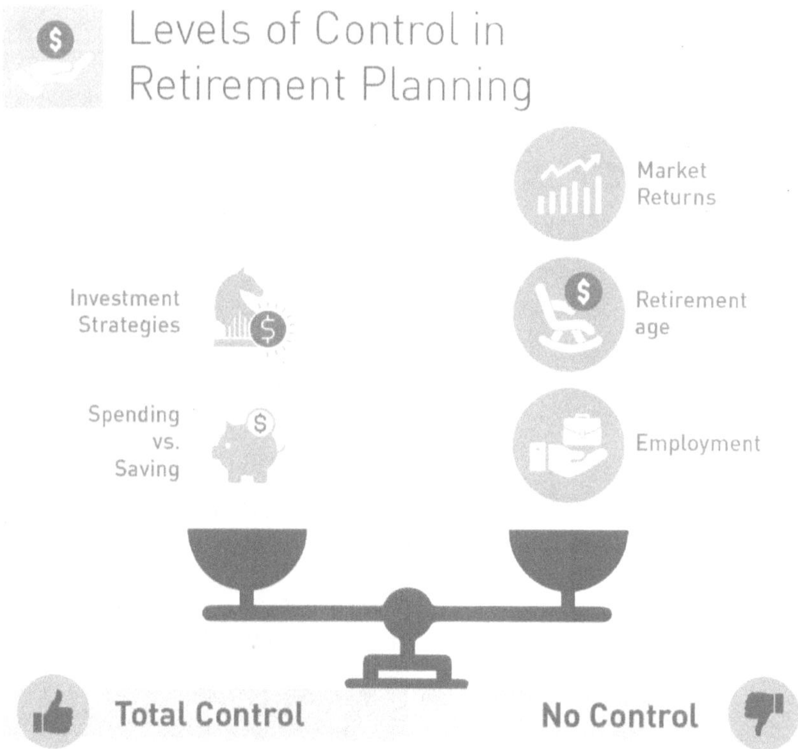
Levels of Control in Retirement Planning
Market Returns
Investment Strategies
Retirement age
Spending vs. Saving
Employment
Total Control
No Control

CHAPTER 4
STEP 3: RETIRE ON YOUR OWN TERMS; KNOW YOUR SOURCES OF INCOME, CLAIMS AND COSTS

"The more you learn, the more you earn."

WARREN BUFFETT

4.1 BLUEPRINT TO SUSTAINABLE INCOME

Our blueprint starts with creating a checklist to fill in any gaps in your understanding. This crucial step empowers you to retire on your terms.

Please take the time to fill out this checklist. It will be very handy as you move through this book and work through where you need to seek additional information on your journey. You may want to check each item off as you learn more and feel confident about making the next decision.

This is about creating multiple streams of income that work together. It gives you the flexibility to handle and protect yourself against unexpected challenges. This approach helps your money last longer through thoughtful tax planning and careful withdrawal strategies while keeping some of it invested for growth. Think of it as having several backup plans instead of putting all your eggs in one basket.

Chapter 4 delves into the essential details of Income, Benefits, Claims, and Tax information, all crucial for attaining Retirement Readiness.

Chapter 5 follows up with Budgeting, Spending and Saving Principles.

Chapter 6 Active Wealth Management and Product Integration takes this knowledge a step further with Investment Principles.

Rest assured, we focus on the essentials to prevent feeling overwhelmed. By simplifying complex information, we lay a foundation for basic retirement planning understanding, giving you the confidence to start. Remember, beginning your journey is crucial. With a grasp of the basics, we recommend then seeking advice from Approved Financial Counsel for guidance tailored to your needs. Often, the biggest hurdle is the first step: stick with us!

Interactive Exercise: Your Retirement Checklist

4.2 CORE INCOME BUILDING BLOCKS: YOUR RETIREMENT INCOME REPLACEMENT NEEDS

Needs vary across different households and income levels:

The percentage of pre-retirement income needed to maintain a similar lifestyle in retirement varies significantly depending on your current household income and history of savings. This variation occurs because often different income levels are associated with distinct saving patterns, spending behaviours, and tax obligations.

For example, lower-income households typically need to replace a higher percentage of their pre-retirement income - often 80-85% or more. This is because:

- They generally save less during their working years due to tighter budgets
- A more significant portion of their income goes toward essential expenses
- They pay lower taxes during their working years, so the tax reduction in Retirement is less significant

In contrast, higher-income households often need to replace a smaller percentage of their pre-retirement income - sometimes as low as 60-65% because:

- They typically save more during their working years
- A more significant portion of their income goes to discretionary spending that may decrease in retirement
- They experience a more substantial drop in taxes during retirement
- They no longer need to save for retirement once they retired

Your Income Replacement Framework

This guidance assumes a household where the primary earner retires at 65 and their spouse at 63. It is a guide and should not be taken as a substitute for Approved Personal Retirement Planning Advice. If current savings fall below or above the recommended amount for your age and income level, consider consulting a financial professional to develop a personalized retirement strategy.

How can I determine the amount I need to save to substitute my current income in retirement?

The guide below provides concrete savings targets, adjustment factors, and implementation steps.

Income Replacement Guidelines for Middle-Income Households ($30,000-$90,000)

- Starting Point: Save 5% of gross income
- Recommended Range: Save 10-15% of gross income (including employer match)
- Optimal Target: Save 15-20% for those starting after age 30

A few key points to highlight:

1. The 5% baseline is really a minimum - most people should aim for 15-20% including employer match
2. Early starting age is crucial - waiting requires significantly higher savings rates
3. Income replacement needs vary but typically range from 70-80% of pre-retirement income

4. The plan needs regular adjustment based on personal circumstances

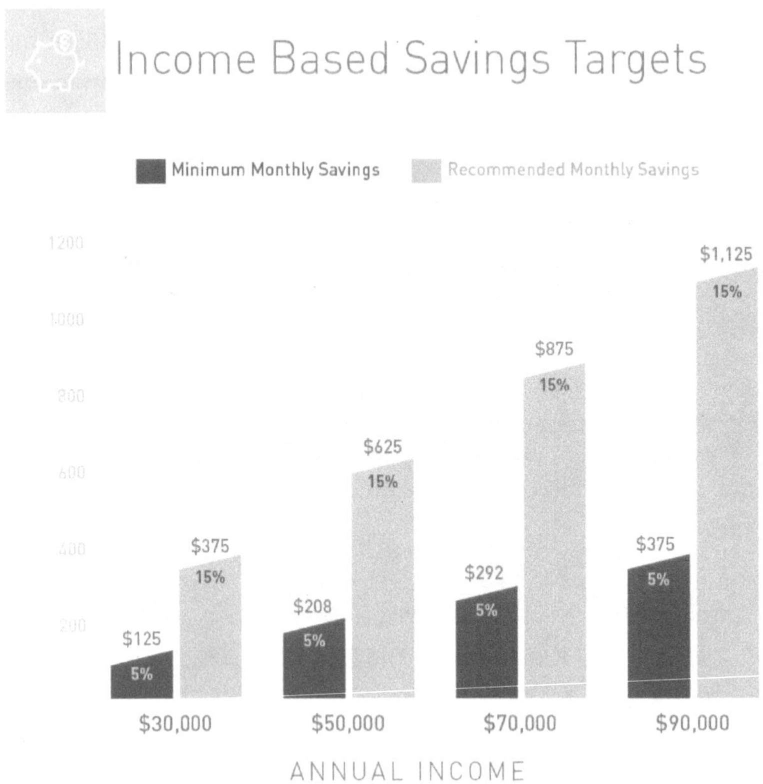

Key Considerations

(i) Income Replacement Needs

- Aim to replace 70-80% of pre-retirement income
- Example calculation at $50,000 salary:
  - Target annual retirement income: $35,000-$40,000
  - Monthly retirement income needed: $2,917-$3,333

(ii) Adjustment Factors

Increase base savings rate if you:

- Start saving after age 30 (+3-5% additional)
- Have high medical expenses (+2-3%)
- Live in a high-cost area (+2-5%)
- Want to retire early (+5-10%)
- Have limited pension/Social Security expectations (+3-5%)

What if I still need to start saving?

Determining the ideal retirement savings plan is highly personal. It varies based on several factors, including income level, the standard of living one wishes to maintain in retirement, and the age at which one begins saving.

A younger individual, say 25 years old, may need to allocate between 5% and 15% of their gross income towards retirement savings—a manageable target with careful financial planning. On the other hand, for someone beginning today to save at age 50, the suggested savings rate jumps significantly, ranging from 15% to 35% of their gross income. This higher rate may pose challenges for many, underlining the advantage of starting the savings journey as early as possible to enhance the likelihood of a comfortable retirement.

Timeline Impact

Starting Age	Required Saving Rate
25	10-15%
35	15-20%
45	20-25%
55	25-30%

*Assuming 6% average annual return, adjusted for inflation

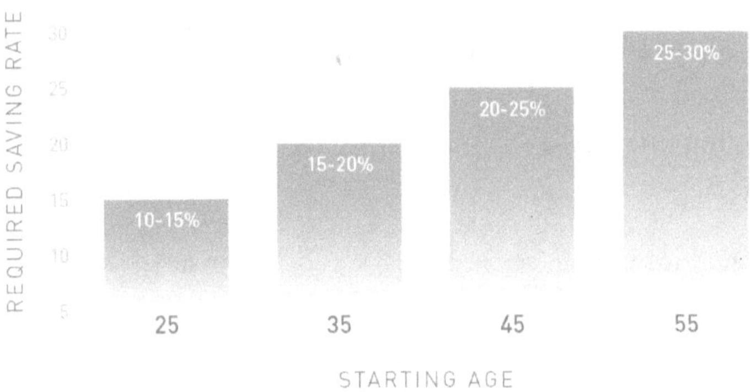

4.3 YOUR SAVING AND INVESTING PATH CAN DRAMATICALLY IMPACT YOUR RETIREMENT NEST EGG

Let's look at how four different approaches play out:

This comparison shows us that how and when you save matters as much as how much you save.

A consistent, long-term investment strategy started early can be more powerful than playing catch-up later or keeping savings in low-yield cash accounts.This chart shows four different retirement saving scenarios from age 20 to 65.

The Power Player: Meet our *consistent investor* who saves and invests regularly throughout their working years. They build the most significant retirement fund of all four scenarios by staying the course from start to finish. *Saves $500/month and invests in the market (7% annual return)*

The Early Bird: This person *front-loads their retirement strategy*, saving and investing aggressively in their early career before stopping completely. Despite contributing only a third of what the late starter invests, their early timing allows compound interest to work its magic, resulting in a larger final balance than the late starter. *Saves $500/month for first 15 years only and invests in the market*

The Late Bloomer: While this person *eventually invests triple* what the early bird contributed, their delayed start means less time for compound growth to work in their favour. Despite higher total contributions, they end up with less than the early bird. *Saves $500/month for the last 15 years only and invests in the market*

The Conservative Keeper: Though this person *saves just as diligently as the consistent investor*, they keep everything in cash rather than investing in growth assets. Without putting their money to work in the market, their savings grow much more slowly, ultimately leaving them with the smallest nest egg despite their disciplined saving habits. *Saves $500/month the entire time but keeps it in cash (2% annual return)*

This demonstrates:

- The power of consistent, long-term investing
- How early investing can outperform late investing even with less total contribution
- The opportunity cost of keeping long-term savings in cash instead of investing

4.4 CORE INCOME BUILDING BLOCKS: SOCIAL SECURITY, PENSIONS AND RMD'S

This section outlines essential elements to Building Retirement Income in the United States.

Social Security base - Provides a more significant percentage of replacement income for lower-income households and represents a smaller portion of total retirement income for higher-income households due to the program's progressive nature.

Pensions & RMDs: Includes 401(k)s, IRAs, pensions, and other retirement accounts.

Account withdrawals: The proportion needed from personal savings increases with pre-retirement income level; higher-income households must rely more heavily on their savings.

Part-time work options - supplement income and stay active.

Unfortunately, many people haven't calculated their retirement needs to maintain their current lifestyle, so they are unsure how to structure these Income-Building Blocks to be Retirement-Ready.

Social Security Timing Trade-offs

Only some Americans understand the benefits and trade-offs of claiming Social Security at various ages. Choosing to delay your Social Security benefits can significantly boost your retirement income. By waiting until age 70 to claim, your monthly benefit can increase by 24-32% compared to claiming at your full retirement age (FRA). Conversely, opting to receive benefits early, at age 62, means your checks will be permanently reduced to 70-75% of the amount you would receive if you waited until your FRA. Moreover, cost-of-living adjustments (COLA) will be applied annually, widening the gap in benefit amounts over time. For instance, the COLA for 2023 was 8.7%, while the average annual COLA over the past 38 years has been around 2.8%. This strategic patience offers immediate financial benefits and ensures a higher income adjusted for inflation throughout your retirement years.

The Social Security Amendments Act of 1983 gradually raised the Full Retirement Age (FRA) from 65 to 67 over four decades. Initially, the FRA increased to 66 for those turning 62 between 2000 and 2005. Following a pause, the FRA then moved from 66 to 67 for individuals, reaching 62 from 2017 to 2022. This overview aims to provide a foundational understanding of Social Security changes and should be different from professional advice. For specific inquiries regarding how these adjustments affect your retirement planning, it's advisable to consult directly with the Social Security Administration or seek guidance from a legal or tax advisor to explore options that maximize your benefits.

Social Security and Working During Retirement

Working during Retirement can affect your Social Security benefits. Suppose you claim benefits before reaching your FRA and continue to work. In that case, the Social Security Administration may reduce your benefits if your earnings exceed certain limits. This reduction is temporary, as once you reach FRA, your benefits will be recalculated to give you credit for the months your benefits were reduced. Understanding how working affects your benefits can help you plan better. Balancing work and retirement income requires careful consideration of these rules. This ensures you make the most of both your earnings and Social Security benefits.

Consider the case of Tom and Linda, a couple who successfully navigated their retirement benefits. Tom, a teacher with a defined benefit pension, chose a monthly payout over a lump sum. This decision provided a stable income, supplementing their other retirement savings. On the other hand, Linda had a 401(k) and decided to continue working part-time after retiring. She carefully monitored her earnings to avoid reducing her Social Security benefits. By coordinating their benefits, they maximized their retirement income. Linda also claimed spousal benefits on Tom's record, increasing their monthly income further. This strategic approach allowed them to enjoy their Retirement without financial worry.

Pension Plans

Pension plans can be a cornerstone of retirement income for many. Understanding how they work is critical to maximizing their benefits. There are two main types: defined benefit and defined contribution plans. A defined benefit plan promises a specific payout upon Retirement. This amount is usually based on your salary and years of service. The employer bears the investment risk, ensuring a steady income.

In contrast, a defined contribution plan, like a 401(k), depends on how much you and your employer contribute. The payout depends on the investment's performance. With these plans, you carry the risk and reward. Choosing between different pension payout options can also impact your income. Options include a lump sum or monthly payments. Each has pros and cons, so consider your financial needs carefully. Evaluating these choices helps align your pension benefits with your lifestyle and financial goals.

Social Security benefits form another crucial part of your retirement income. Timing your claim can significantly impact your benefits.

You can start claiming as early as 62, but waiting until your full retirement age (FRA) or even later can increase your monthly payments. Each year you delay past your FRA, your benefits increase. Spousal and survivor benefits offer additional strategies. If you're married, you might be eligible for spousal benefits, up to half of your partner's benefit. Survivor benefits can also provide income if your spouse passes away. These benefits can be complex, but understanding them can help you make informed decisions.

Required Minimum Distributions (RMD's)

Understanding Required Minimum Distributions (RMDs) becomes crucial as you enter Retirement. RMDs are mandatory withdrawals from your retirement accounts. They start when you reach a certain age. The government requires these withdrawals to ensure taxes are eventually paid on tax-deferred savings. If you have a Traditional IRA or a 401(k), you must begin taking RMDs at age 73. Each year, you must withdraw a specific amount. Failing to do so results in hefty penalties. The penalty is 50% of the amount you should have withdrawn but didn't. This can significantly impact your savings. Therefore, staying informed about RMD rules is essential for maintaining financial health.

When it comes to managing RMDs, planning is vital. One strategy is to use these distributions to cover living expenses. This way, you align your required withdrawals with your financial needs, turning a mandatory action into a beneficial one. Another option is to direct RMDs toward charitable giving. Consider a Qualified Charitable Distribution (QCD) if you are charitably inclined. This allows you to transfer up to $100,000 directly from your IRA to a charity. This transfer satisfies your RMD requirement but does not count as taxable income. This can be a powerful tool for both meeting your distribution requirements and supporting causes you care about.

Calculating your RMD can seem complex, but it's manageable. The IRS provides tables to help determine the amount you must withdraw each year. These tables consider your age and your retirement account balance as of December 31 of the previous year. The calculation involves dividing your account balance by a life expectancy factor in these tables. For example, if your account balance is $100,000 and the factor is 25.6, your RMD would be approximately $3,906. This calculation must be done annually, as your account balance and age change each year. Understanding this process ensures you withdraw the correct amount and avoid penalties.

RMDs also have tax implications. Withdrawals increase your taxable income, which can affect your tax bracket. This increase might lead to a higher tax bill, reducing the net amount you receive. Planning your RMDs with tax efficiency in mind is essential. Consider how RMDs will impact your overall tax situation. Strategically withdrawing funds can minimize the tax impact. For instance, if you have other sources of income, you might plan withdrawals in years when your income is lower. This can help you stay in a lower tax bracket. Being aware of these implications allows you to manage your retirement funds wisely.

To summarize, understanding RMDs is a vital part of retirement planning. They ensure you take the necessary steps to comply with tax regulations while managing your financial needs. Incorporating RMDs into your financial plan allows you to turn them from a requirement into an opportunity. Whether it's funding your lifestyle or supporting your favourite charities, RMDs can be used effectively to enhance your retirement experience. Calculating the exact amounts using IRS tables and planning for tax impacts can help you maximise your savings. Staying informed and proactive will serve you well as you navigate these financial waters.

4.5 CORE INCOME BUILDING BLOCKS: DEMYSTIFYING TAX-EFFICIENT ACCOUNT WITHDRAWALS FROM YOUR EARNINGS

Understanding how taxes affect your retirement withdrawals can significantly affect how long your savings last. Each type of account—like a Traditional IRA, Roth IRA, or 401(k)—has its own tax rules. With a Traditional IRA, you pay taxes when you withdraw money. This means these withdrawals are added to your annual income, possibly increasing your tax bracket. In contrast, with a Roth IRA, you've already paid taxes on your contributions. Withdrawals here are tax-free, which can be a significant advantage when managing your retirement income. For 401(k) accounts, withdrawals are taxed as ordinary income, similar to Traditional IRAs. The key is understanding these differences so you can plan your withdrawals strategically.

Timing your withdrawals is crucial for minimizing taxes. Drawing money to keep your total income in a lower tax bracket can save you a lot over time. For example, you might withdraw from a Roth IRA in a year when your income is higher, avoiding extra taxes since those withdrawals don't count as income. Another strategy involves converting a Traditional IRA to a Roth IRA. This is known as a Roth conversion. It involves paying taxes on the converted amount now but allows for tax-free withdrawals later. This can be beneficial if you expect your future tax rate to be higher. These decisions should align with your broader retirement strategy.

The sequence you withdraw from your various accounts also affects your tax liabilities. Generally, it's wise to tap into taxable accounts first. This allows the tax-deferred accounts to continue growing. Next, consider withdrawing from tax-deferred accounts like a Traditional IRA or 401(k). Lastly, use tax-free accounts like a Roth IRA. This sequence can help extend your savings life by minimizing the impact of taxes. It also allows you to take advantage of the compounding growth in your tax-advantaged accounts for as long as possible.

Consider the real-life example of Clara, a retiree who managed her withdrawals smartly. Clara first withdrew from her taxable investment account, using the lower capital gains tax rate to her advantage. She then gradually converted portions of her Traditional IRA to a Roth IRA during years when her income was lower. This allowed her to pay taxes on the conversions at a lower rate. By the time she needed to dip into her tax-deferred accounts, she had already reduced the balance, which lowered her required minimum distributions. This careful strategy minimized her tax burden and maximized her retirement savings.

Real-world examples like Clara's show how tax-efficient withdrawal strategies can make a big difference. Planning your withdrawals with an eye on taxes can help you keep more of your money. It's about being bright with when and how much you withdraw from each account. This approach requires looking ahead and sometimes making tough choices, but the payoff can be significant. With the right strategy, you can stretch your savings further and enjoy a more comfortable retirement.

4.5 INCOME PROTECTION STRATEGY: UNDERSTANDING YOUR INDIVIDUAL HEALTHCARE SITUATION

Imagine sitting down with a stack of mail, only to find each envelope filled with terms like "Part A," "Medigap," and "Advantage Plans." For many over 50, understanding Medicare can feel overwhelming. Yet, it's a crucial step in securing your healthcare during Retirement. This section will break down Medicare into simple parts, making it easier to navigate and understand.

Medicare is divided into four parts, each covering different services. Part A is hospital insurance. It helps pay for inpatient stays, skilled nursing facility care, and home healthcare. Most people don't pay a premium for Part A if they or their spouse paid Medicare taxes while working. Part B covers medical insurance. It includes doctor visits, outpatient care, and preventive services. You pay a monthly premium for Part B, which can vary based on your income. Together, Parts A and B are known as Original Medicare.

Medicare Advantage Plans, or Part C, offer an alternative to Original Medicare. Private companies approved by Medicare provides these plans. They combine Part A and Part B coverage, often including additional benefits like vision, hearing, and dental. Some plans also include Part D, which covers prescription drugs. While Medicare Advantage plans can offer more services, they may also have network restrictions and different costs. Carefully consider your health needs and preferences before choosing.

Part D is prescription drug coverage. It helps cover the cost of medications and is available through private companies. You can add Part D to Original Medicare or get it through a Medicare Advantage plan. Each plan varies in cost and covered drugs, so comparing options during the annual open enrollment period is essential. This period runs from October 15 to December 7 each year. During this time, you can make changes to your Medicare coverage.

Enrolling in Medicare requires meeting specific timelines. Your initial enrollment period begins three months before your 65th birthday and ends three months after. Missing this window could lead to penalties or delayed coverage. However, there are special enrollment periods. These allow you to sign up without penalties if you have certain life events, like losing employer coverage. Knowing your eligibility and timelines ensures you can meet important deadlines.

Medicare doesn't cover everything, which is where supplemental insurance, or Medigap, comes in. Medigap helps pay for costs not covered by Original Medicare, like copayments, coinsurance, and deductibles. Unlike Medicare Advantage, Medigap policies don't include extra benefits like dental or vision. You pay a separate premium for Medigap. When choosing between Medigap and Medicare Advantage, consider your healthcare needs, preferred doctors, and budget.

Checklist for Choosing Medicare Plans

- Assess Your Healthcare Needs: Consider your current and future health requirements. Do you need specific specialists or medications?
- Compare Costs: Look at premiums, deductibles, and out-of-pocket maximums. Which plan offers the best value for your situation?
- Check Provider Networks: If you prefer certain doctors or hospitals, ensure they're included in the plan's network.
- Evaluate Extra Benefits: Decide if additional services like dental or vision are essential to you.

- Review Drug Coverage: Ensure the plan covers your prescriptions and look at pharmacy options.

Use this checklist to guide your decision-making process. It will help you choose the Medicare plan that best fits your needs and lifestyle. Remember, the right plan provides coverage and peace of mind as you focus on enjoying your Retirement.

Evaluating Health Insurance Costs and Options in Retirement

As you approach retirement, evaluating your health insurance options becomes crucial. While Medicare provides a foundation, you may find that additional coverage is necessary to meet all your needs. Comparing private insurance with Medicare is an important step. Private insurance can offer broader coverage or extra benefits that Medicare does not include, such as dental or vision care. However, it often comes at a higher cost. Weighing these costs against the benefits helps determine if private insurance is worth the extra expense. Consider your health history, current needs, and future expectations. Private insurance might be beneficial if you anticipate frequent visits to specialists or need specific medications not covered by Medicare. However, sticking with Medicare and possibly a supplemental plan could suffice if you have minimal healthcare needs.

Employer-sponsored retiree health benefits are key in insurance planning. Some employers offer these benefits, which can save money and offer comprehensive coverage. It's important to understand how these benefits work with Medicare to prevent any coverage overlaps or gaps. Review your employer's plan to ensure it complements Medicare, especially in areas Medicare might not cover, maximizing the benefits of both plans. This approach can considerably lower out-of-pocket costs and offer additional peace of mind.

A Health Savings Account (HSA) offers a smart way to manage healthcare costs in retirement with three key tax benefits: tax-deductible contributions, tax-deferred growth, and tax-free withdrawals for qualified medical expenses. Eligibility for an HSA requires enrollment in a High Deductible Health Plan (HDHP). Even after you switch to Medicare, you can still use your HSA funds for eligible expenses, including Medicare premiums and long-term care. An HSA helps protect your retirement savings from healthcare expenses.

In retirement, your health insurance needs can change over time. Regularly reviewing your coverage and options ensures you remain protected as those needs evolve. Staying informed about changes in insurance policies and healthcare laws is crucial. This knowledge helps you adapt your Plan as necessary, maintaining the best coverage at the most reasonable cost.

Strategies for Managing Rising Healthcare Costs

Healthcare costs significantly impact retirees, with expenses expected to increase as they age. Proactively managing these costs is vital for financial stability and ensuring access to necessary medical care. Implementing early strategies can prevent savings from being quickly depleted. Utilizing preventative care through regular check-ups and screenings can identify health issues early, potentially avoiding costly treatments for severe conditions. Most insurance plans cover vaccinations and routine tests, making preventative care an affordable option for maintaining health. Adopting a healthy lifestyle with a balanced diet and regular exercise can also reduce healthcare costs by preventing health problems. Additionally, negotiating medical bills can lead to savings, as many don't realize these costs are often negotiable. Hospitals may offer discounts or payment plans to alleviate financial stress. Leveraging community resources is another strategy to manage healthcare expenses effectively. Local health clinics and non-profit organizations often provide services at reduced costs or even for free, offering valuable support and helping to minimize financial burdens. Researching available resources in your area can connect you to services that suit your healthcare needs and assist in managing rising costs.

4.6 INCOME PROTECTION STRATEGY: PLANNING FOR LONG-TERM CARE WITHOUT BREAKING THE BANK

Planning for Long-Term Care: A Must for Financial Security As we age, the likelihood of requiring long-term care increases significantly. With nearly 70% of individuals over 65 needing such care, the associated costs can pose a serious threat to your savings. Ranging from home aides at approximately $33 per hour to private nursing home rooms at $9,733 monthly, these expenses necessitate early financial preparation. Long-Term Care Insurance: A Viable Solution To mitigate these costs, consider long-term care insurance, which covers services like in-home care, assisted living, and nursing home stays. These policies vary, offering options like inflation protection to maintain benefit relevance over time. However, premiums can rise with age. Alternatively, hybrid policies blend life insurance with long-term care benefits, providing flexibility and ensuring that unused premiums benefit your heirs. Alternative Funding Strategies: Beyond Insurance For those ineligible or preferring not to opt for insurance, leveraging home equity through a reverse mortgage can provide necessary funds without selling your home. Yet, this reduces inheritance equity. Establishing a dedicated savings account for long-term care is another strategy, demanding discipline but offering a safety net without insurance reliance. Medicaid: The Safety Net with Caveats As a last resort, Medicaid covers long-term care for individuals with limited assets and income. The eligibility criteria are stringent, often requiring asset depletion to qualify. Though a crucial option for some, Medicaid's limitations on care facility choices and the complexity of its spend-down rules underscore the importance of consulting financial advisors or attorneys. Planning with these considerations in mind ensures both financial stability and peace of mind for your future care needs.

Case Study: Choosing the Right Long-term Care Plan

Consider Jane, a retired teacher who planned for long-term care. She weighed her options carefully. Jane decided on a hybrid policy to cover potential care needs. She liked that the policy offered a death benefit if she didn't use the care coverage. This reassured her that her premiums wouldn't be wasted. Jane also set aside some savings in a dedicated account. This gave her flexibility and control over her funds. She consulted with a financial advisor to understand Medicaid's rules and adjusted her Plan to protect some assets. Jane's approach gave her peace of mind and economic security. It showed how preparation and understanding options can lead to a solid plan.

4.7 INCOME PROTECTION STRATEGY: EMERGENCY FUND TO BUILD FINANCIAL RESILIENCE

The Retirement Confidence Survey identifies the top three reasons individuals tap into their 401(k) plans through loans or withdrawals. These include settling credit card debt, managing medical bills, and handling emergency costs. This underscores the importance of emergency savings.

Although many of us aspire to extend our careers later in life, circumstances may only sometimes permit this. A significant portion of workers anticipate remaining employed until 65 or beyond; however, the reality for many retirees tells a different story. About a third report retiring sooner than planned, often due to unforeseen health issues, disabilities, or shifts within their companies. This disparity underscores the importance of having a financial safety net. Securing disability insurance is crucial, particularly for those whose livelihoods rely on continued income.

Everyday unexpected expenses to prepare for:

- Medical emergencies and procedures
- Home repairs and maintenance
- Vehicle replacements or major repairs
- Family emergencies
- Natural disasters or other unexpected events

Building a robust financial foundation for Retirement requires having a cushion against the unexpected. Life's unpredictability—from sudden car repairs to job loss or reduced work hours—underscores the necessity of emergency savings. Without a financial safety net, there's a risk of dipping into retirement funds prematurely, jeopardizing future financial security. The appropriate size of an emergency fund varies and is influenced by income, personal circumstances, and individual comfort levels.

A useful benchmark is to save 2-3 months' worth of salary for those still working and 3-6 months' worth for retirees, who may face more frequent and significant unplanned expenses, especially related to healthcare. Households with lower incomes should aim for larger emergency funds, as any financial shock can substantially hit their regular spending.

The absence of an emergency savings fund can seriously affect your readiness for Retirement. 90% of employees face considerable spending increases, at least 25% above their usual spending within a year. Alarmingly, one-third of these individuals cannot cover these unexpected expenses with their savings, leading to a reliance on credit cards or borrowing against their 401(k) plans. This situation underscores the critical importance of building and maintaining a robust emergency fund to safeguard your financial stability in retirement.

CHAPTER 5
STEP 4: THE SPENDING V SAVINGS JUGGLE

"The foundation of wealth building isn't about the money you make, but rather the habits you create to keep and multiply what you earn."

SUZE ORMAN

Achieving a financially secure retirement is a more intricate journey than many anticipate, mainly due to the unpredictable nature of retirement timing and various risk factors.

Timing Uncertainty The most striking revelation is that retirement timing often isn't a personal choice. EBRI's research shows that approximately 50% of workers are forced into retirement prematurely due to circumstances beyond their control, such as health issues or corporate restructuring. This unpredictability makes financial planning significantly more challenging.

The prospect of outliving our savings is a widespread concern. By becoming more prepared for retirement, we can significantly reduce the likelihood of this becoming our reality. Let's examine FOUR common risk factors that threaten our retirement savings.

While some of these risks are beyond our control, understanding them better equips us to craft a more resilient retirement plan.

Risk One: Market Volatility Impact

The timing of investment returns plays a pivotal role when you start taking money out of your retirement savings. Experiencing a downturn in the market just as you enter retirement can significantly impact your financial stability for years to come. Additionally, if you're buying an annuity to provide a steady income during retirement, doing so when interest rates are low can result in receiving lower monthly payments than you might have at higher interest rates.

Risk Two: The Longevity Puzzle

Retirement planning involves navigating a crucial balance: Being overly cautious can lead to unnecessarily limiting your lifestyle and possibly leaving behind more assets than intended. On the other hand, being too bold could result in spending all your savings too early. Achieving the proper equilibrium is especially difficult because predicting how long we'll live is hard.

Risk Three: Inflation's Hidden Threat

Social Security offers some protection against Inflation, ensuring that your income keeps up, to some extent, with the rising cost of living. However, your payments from a fixed annuity might have different safeguarding effects. Over time, these payments might stretch farther than they used to, leading to a growing discrepancy between your income and your daily costs.

Risk Four: Dynamic Spending Patterns

What makes this especially interesting is how retirement spending isn't static, as many assume. We often see a counterintuitive pattern:

- Age 65: Retirees need 92% of pre-retirement income
- Age 85: This drops to 70%

However, unexpected medical costs or life events can disrupt this general trend.

5.1 CREATING A SUSTAINABLE RETIREMENT BUDGET: YOUR GUIDE

Understanding Your Financial Canvas

Crafting a retirement budget is like painting a picture of your future life – each brushstroke represents a decision that shapes your financial landscape. The key to creating this masterpiece is understanding your current financial patterns and anticipating future needs.

At the foundation of financial management lies a simple yet crucial principle: income must exceed spending to be prepared for retirement. Despite this concept's straightforwardness, many people spend beyond their means, leading to significant debt and financial stress.

We have provided you with the key Steps for your Basic Financial Canvas. This is where you combine all the information we have laid out so far. You can always go back to re-read any chapter at any time. This is where the rubber hits the road.

Interactive Exercise: Your Financial Canvas

Step 1: Revisit Your Retirement Checklist from the previous chapter. Check off the key areas you now understand better.

Step 2: Your Current Financial Situation

Create a spreadsheet in Excel or other format to your liking. Make a column with a list of the following headings and subheadings.

- Income Sources: Social Security, pensions, savings withdrawals
- Essential Expenses (Needs): Housing (mortgage/rent), Utilities (electricity, water, gas, internet), Groceries, Healthcare (Insurance Premiums, Regular Medication), Property taxes, Transportation (car payments, fuel, maintenance)
- Discretionary Expenses: Travel & Vacations, Dining out, Hobbies, Entertainment, Gifts, Charitable Donations, Optional subscriptions and memberships
- Emergency Fund Goal: Three to six months of essential expenses

You may adjust the categories to fit your personal needs and lifestyle.

Track your current expenses meticulously for the last 3-6 months. Insert Spend in the Column to the Right of this list.

Most banks will allow you to export your statements into an Excel format. This will help you to aggregate all of your transactions in one place. From here you can start to label, highlight and categorise.

Step 3: Planning for Tomorrow

Create a separate spreadsheet with the same headings and subheadings as outlined for Step 2 above. Label this sheet "Planning for Tomorrow"

Revisit the Objectives you set out in your action plan from Chapter 2. Insert the required dollar amounts for each of these subheadings required to achieve your PACT objectives.

Consider how your lifestyle might change in retirement:

- Will you travel more frequently? How much is your travel going to cost you?
- Do you plan to pursue new hobbies? How much new investment are your new hobbies going to need
- Might you relocate to a different area? What is the cost of moving house or downsizing?
- Would you like to spend more time on family activities?
- What is the cost of Nursing and medical care you may need
- What are the long-term costs of health care or life insurance?
- And any other changes you can foresee

Step 4: Schedule quarterly budget reviews to

- Compare actual spending against projections.
- Identify areas needing adjustment.
- Update financial goals
- Account for inflation impacts
- Reassess investment returns and withdrawal rates.

While a basic spreadsheet is an excellent tool, remember that numerous online budgeting applications can offer enhanced features should you seek additional functionalities. These may include automatic expense tracking, bill payment reminders, updates on investment fluctuations, customizable budget categories, insights into your spending habits, and progress tracking towards your financial milestones.

Also, look for a user-friendly interface for seniors, large text and clear visuals, secure data encryption, multi-device synchronization, export capabilities for tax preparation, and integration with financial institutions.

5.2 TIPS FOR SUCCESS

1. Start Early: Begin tracking expenses at least 2-3 years before retirement
2. Be Realistic: Don't underestimate costs or overestimate income
3. Build Buffers: Include padding in each category for unexpected increases
4. Stay Flexible: Maintain a willingness to adjust as circumstances change
5. Seek Guidance: Consider working with a financial advisor for personalized strategies
6. Monitor and Adjust: Regular review and refinement of your budget is essential
7. Stay Informed: Keep up with financial news and retirement planning trends

Remember, your retirement budget is a living document that should evolve with you. Regular reviews and adjustments ensure it continues to serve your needs while maintaining financial security throughout your retirement years.

5.3 MAXIMIZING YOUR NEST EGG: SAVINGS STRATEGIES FOR LONGEVITY

Before retirement, consider ways to increase your savings. If you are over 50, you can make catch-up contributions to your retirement accounts. This is an opportunity to boost your savings significantly. For instance, you can contribute extra to your 401(k) or IRA. Automating your savings can also enhance discipline. Set up automatic transfers from your paycheck or bank account to your retirement fund. This ensures you consistently save and takes the guesswork out of the process. Each small contribution adds up over time, especially when combined with the power of compounding.

Compounding is a powerful ally in retirement savings. It allows your money to grow, not just on your initial investment but also on the earnings it generates. The earlier you start saving, the more time compounding has to work magic. Even small amounts can grow into substantial savings over the years. Consistency is key. Regular contributions, no matter how small, can lead to significant growth. Over time, your savings can multiply, building a solid nest egg for your retirement.

One of the most effective ways to protect your savings is through diversification. This means spreading your investments across different types of assets. Think of it as not putting all your eggs in one basket. Investing in a mix of stocks, bonds, and alternative investments reduces your risk.

Think of retirement savings like having different piggy banks with special tax rules. Just like you would want to keep only some of your money in one place, you want to avoid all your retirement savings taxing the same way. Here's why:

Different Types of Retirement Savings "Piggy Banks"

- Traditional Retirement Accounts (like 401(k)s and Traditional IRAs)
  - You receive a tax benefit upon depositing money; however, taxes apply upon withdrawal during retirement—it's akin to enjoying a discount upfront but facing the regular cost down the line.
- Roth Accounts (Roth IRA, Roth 401(k))
  - You pay taxes on the money before putting it in. But then you never pay taxes again! Like paying total price now but getting everything free later
- Regular Investment Accounts
  - You pay taxes on any earnings each year. Like paying a little bit as you go
- Health Savings Accounts (HSAs)
  - Triple tax advantage: tax break when you put money in, grows tax-free, and tax-free withdrawals for medical expenses. Like getting a discount now AND later for healthcare costs

5.4 WHY DIFFERENT TYPES OF SAVINGS APPROACHES MATTER IN RETIREMENT

Your retirement income sources can significantly impact your tax bill and healthcare costs. Regarding Social Security, earning more taxable income might mean paying taxes on a more significant portion of your benefits. However, you can reduce this tax burden by drawing from tax-free sources like Roth accounts. This strategy also helps with Medicare costs since higher income levels can increase your premiums, but tax-free withdrawals don't count toward these income limits. Think of having different retirement accounts like having a financial toolbox – you can choose which "tool" (account) to use based on your specific needs each year, helping you manage your tax situation more effectively. This flexibility allows you to adapt your withdrawal strategy as your circumstances change throughout retirement.

Real-Life Example:

Imagine you need $50,000 for expenses one year in retirement:

- Option 1: Take it all from a traditional IRA (might push you into a higher tax bracket)
- Option 2: Take $30,000 from a traditional IRA and $20,000 from a Roth (might keep you in a lower tax bracket)
- Option 3: Mix and match from different accounts based on your needs

So, Where do I start?

1. Start with your workplace retirement plan (usually a 401(k))
2. Consider opening a Roth IRA
3. If eligible, look into an HSA for healthcare savings
4. Save some money in regular investment accounts
5. Don't worry about getting it perfect - just starting with different types of accounts is a good move!

Remember:

- You don't need to understand all the complex tax rules
- The key is to have different types of accounts available
- This gives you more control over your taxes in retirement
- It's like giving your future self more options!

5.5 A STEP FURTHER: UNDERSTANDING ANNUITIES

Imagine sitting down with a cup of coffee, flipping through your finances. You see your savings, pensions, and investments lined up. But something is missing. A steady, reliable source of income. This is where annuities come into play. They promise to turn your savings into a predictable income stream. For many over 50, this can be a way to secure a stable financial future. Annuities are contracts with a life insurance company. They offer guaranteed payments over time. This can provide peace of mind and help fund your retirement lifestyle.

Annuities come in several types, each with its benefits and drawbacks. Fixed annuities are the simplest. They offer a guaranteed rate of return over a set period. This provides predictable income, which can be a relief. But be wary of Inflation. It can erode the purchasing power of the fixed payouts over time. Variable annuities, on the other hand, link your income to the performance of investments. This offers the growth potential but also comes with risk. Your payouts can fluctuate, and you may face high fees. Indexed annuities are another option. They tie your returns to a market index like the S&P 500. They protect your principal from loss, but gains may be capped. Each type of annuity has its own rules and conditions, which makes understanding them essential before making a choice.

Annuities offer the advantage of guaranteed income. This can complement other income sources like Social Security. Having a consistent monthly check can make budgeting more accessible and reduce financial stress. Yet, they are not without downsides. Fees can be high, eating into your returns. Surrender charges can apply if you withdraw early. These penalties can be steep. Before purchasing an annuity, weigh these costs against the benefits. Consider if the security of a steady income outweighs the potential expenses. Annuities are complex products, and their long-term commitment requires careful thought.

To decide if an annuity suits you, evaluate your risk tolerance and income needs. Fixed annuities fit well if you prefer steady, predictable income and are risk-averse. Variable annuities could be appealing for those comfortable with market risks and seeking growth. Consider how an annuity might affect your financial liquidity. Once you purchase one, accessing the principal can be challenging due to fees. Ensure you have other funds available for emergencies or unexpected expenses.

Moving Past the Annuity Puzzle

Annuities are often considered a safeguard for retirees, protecting against the dual uncertainties of outliving one's resources and fluctuating markets. Despite these advantages, many individuals hesitate to invest in annuities, a phenomenon experts call the annuity puzzle. This hesitancy stems from a couple of crucial concerns: - Mortality risk pooling means that if an annuity purchaser passes away earlier than the life expectancy models predict, they don't directly benefit from their investment. Instead, their contributions bolster the payouts for those who live longer. This mechanism ensures that no individual outlives their savings. Yet, it can make the initial purchase seem like a gamble on one's lifespan. - The timing of an annuity purchase locks in the income it will generate, offering a shield against downturns in the market. However, it also excludes the investor from potential market gains, which might lead to regrets if the market performs well. Seeking advice from a financial advisor is advisable to understand how an annuity might integrate into a broader retirement strategy, balancing these considerations with your financial goals and needs.

MAKE A DIFFERENCE WITH YOUR REVIEW

EMPOWER OTHERS TO BUILD THEIR FINANCIAL LEGACY

> *"The greatest gift you can give someone is the gift of financial peace of mind."*

Together we can strengthen the financial future of our communities by sharing essential retirement knowledge. Your experience matters.

Would you help someone just like you—worried about their retirement future and looking for clear, trustworthy guidance?

My mission is to make retirement planning simple and achievable for everyone, no matter their starting point. But to reach more people who need this information, I need your help.

Most people choose books based on reviews. So, I'm asking you to help a fellow retirement planner by leaving a review.

It costs nothing and takes less than a minute, but could change someone's financial future. Your review could help...

...one more family create a secure retirement plan ...one more person understand their Medicare options ...one more couple protect their savings from inflation ...one more retiree feel confident about their future ...one more dream retirement come true.

To make a difference, simply scan the QR code below and leave a review:

If you believe everyone deserves a secure retirement, you're my kind of person. Thank you from the bottom of my heart!

===========

Pierce Sullivan

CHAPTER 6
STEP 5: GROWTH FOCUSED INVESTMENT PLANNING

"The majority of millionaires aren't the ones driving fancy cars and living in big houses. They're the ones who live below their means, invest wisely, and focus on wealth preservation."

THOMAS J. STANLEY (AUTHOR OF "THE MILLIONAIRE NEXT DOOR")

Congratulations on this milestone! You've learned a lot. Next, we dive into investment diversification strategies, ensuring they match your portfolio goals. If you're ready, feel free to read ahead. If not you can skip to Chapter 7; Holistic Retirement Planning - Beyond the Financials. Mastering Chapter 1- Chapter 5 already sets a solid foundation for your retirement plan.

6.1 DIVERSIFYING YOUR PORTFOLIO FOR STABILITY

The Three-Bucket System offers a strategic approach to organizing your financial life across different time horizons.

The first bucket consists of cash and highly liquid assets, designed to cover your needs for the next one to two years, ensuring peace of mind for immediate expenses.

Moving further out, the second bucket holds mixed investments spanning three to ten years, striking a balance between growth and stability.

The final bucket takes a growth-focused approach for assets you won't need for at least a decade, allowing you to capitalize on long-term market opportunities without the pressure of short-term volatility.

Imagine your retirement savings as a garden. If you plant all your seeds in one spot and a storm hits, you risk losing everything. But if you spread your seeds across the garden, some will thrive even if others do not. This is the essence of diversification. Diversification helps balance risk and reward, creating a more stable financial picture. It is a crucial strategy for anyone looking to protect and grow their savings.

The main advantage of a diversified portfolio is reduced volatility. When you have a mix of investments, you are less likely to experience significant swings in value. Stocks might drop, but bonds or real estate could hold steady or rise. This balance helps smooth out the bumps, making your portfolio more resilient. Over time, diversification can lead to more stable returns. You might not see huge gains quickly, but slow and steady growth can be more reliable. This approach helps protect your savings from sudden losses.

It also lets you sleep better at night, knowing your investments are spread across different areas.

Let's look at some examples of diversified portfolios for different risk appetites. A conservative portfolio might include 50% bonds, 30% stocks, and 20% real estate. This mix prioritizes stability and income. It is ideal for those who want to preserve capital and avoid significant risks. An aggressive portfolio could have 70% stocks, 20% bonds, and 10% real estate. This setup aims for higher returns and suits those willing to take on more risk. It offers more significant growth potential but comes with increased volatility. Each portfolio reflects a different balance of risk and return, catering to various financial goals and comfort levels.

Maintaining a diversified portfolio requires ongoing attention. This might involve selling one asset to buy another or rebalancing your allocations. Staying informed about your investments helps ensure they continue to meet your needs. Diversification is not a one-time task but an ongoing process. It is about making thoughtful choices to protect and grow your savings. You can create a stable and resilient portfolio that supports your retirement goals with the right mix of assets. Please contact an Approved Financial Advisor.

6.2 MANAGING MARKET VOLATILITY IN RETIREMENT

Market volatility can feel like a rollercoaster. Just when you think your retirement savings are secure, the markets take a dip. For retirees, this can be especially worrying. Your portfolio's value can change rapidly, and you may feel unsure about your financial future. One key concern is the sequence of returns risk. This refers to the order in which your investment returns occur during withdrawal phases. If you experience poor returns early in retirement, it can significantly impact how long your savings last. This is because you might need to withdraw more funds when the market is down, leaving less money to recover when the market rebounds. Understanding this risk can help you plan withdrawals more carefully, ensuring your savings last longer.

To protect your investments from market swings, consider using dollar-cost averaging. This involves regularly investing a fixed amount into your portfolio, regardless of market conditions. By doing so, you buy more shares when prices are low and fewer when prices are high. Over time, this can lower the average cost per share, reducing the risk of investing a large sum just before a market drop. Another strategy is to use stop-loss orders. These automatically sell a security when its price falls to a certain level. Setting stop-loss orders helps limit potential losses by exiting investments before they drop further. Both strategies can buffer against market volatility, ensuring you only lose what you can afford.

Maintaining a long-term perspective is crucial when facing market volatility. It's easy to panic when you see your portfolio's value drop. Still, history shows that markets tend to recover over time. Look at historical market patterns. Despite downturns, the market has generally trended upward over the long run. Keeping this in mind can help you stay calm and focused on your long-term goals. Avoid making hasty decisions based on short-term fluctuations. Instead, stick to your Plan and remember why you invested in the first place. A steady approach can help you weather the storm and come out stronger on the other side.

Consider the case of George and Mary, retirees who adjusted their asset allocation during a market downturn. They noticed their portfolio had become too heavily weighted in stocks, leading to significant losses. Concerned about their financial future, they decided to rebalance their portfolio. They shifted some investments into more stable bonds and cash reserves. This move provided them with a buffer against further market declines. Knowing their essential expenses were covered also gave them peace of mind. By focusing on their long-term Plan and making strategic adjustments, George and Mary navigated the volatility successfully. They avoided the temptation to sell everything in a panic, preserving their savings for the future.

Managing market volatility involves a careful balance of strategy and patience. You can protect your investments by understanding the risks and using tools like dollar-cost averaging and stop-loss orders. Keeping a long-term perspective helps you avoid rash decisions during turbulent times. Learning from others who have successfully navigated volatile markets can also help you gain confidence in your own approach. With the right strategies, you can maintain stability in your retirement portfolio, ensuring your financial security no matter what the markets do.

6.3 AVOIDING COMMON INVESTMENT MISTAKES

Retirement amplifies the importance of financial decisions. A common pitfall is chasing after high-return investments without considering the associated high risks, which can lead to significant losses. Equally, reacting hastily to market news and selling investments during downturns can crystallize losses and miss out on potential recoveries. Markets fluctuate, but historically, they trend upwards over time. Developing a clear investment strategy is critical to navigate these challenges. A strategic plan, aligned with your financial goals and risk tolerance, offers a roadmap for decision-making, helping to avoid emotional reactions to market volatility. It keeps your focus on long-term objectives. Conducting regular portfolio reviews is also crucial. These reviews, ideally at six-month or annual intervals, ensure your investments remain in sync with your goals. As life circumstances and financial markets change, adjustments to your portfolio may be necessary to maintain its balance and effectiveness.

Seeking professional advice is the best course of action. Knowing when to consult with an investment professional can save you from costly mistakes. Complex situations, such as changes in tax laws or significant life events, require expert input. These professionals bring valuable insights and strategies to the table. They can help you understand intricate financial products or navigate uncertain markets. Choosing the right advisor involves checking their credentials and ensuring they know your financial goals. A good advisor acts as a partner, helping you make informed decisions that support your financial well-being.

Avoiding common investment mistakes involves being informed and prepared. You can protect your investments by understanding the risks, sticking to your strategy, and conducting regular reviews. Seeking professional advice when needed ensures you have the guidance to make the best choices. Investing for retirement is a long-term endeavour. Staying patient and focused on your goals can lead to a more secure and fulfilling retirement.

As you continue to explore the world of investments and financial planning, it's crucial to integrate these lessons into your broader retirement strategy. The next chapter will delve into estate planning and legacy, ensuring you build wealth and secure it for future generations. By understanding investment strategies and estate planning, you can create a comprehensive plan supporting your financial goals and personal values.

6.4 INVESTMENTS - KEY QUESTION TEST

Stable Spending Essential Question - What is your monthly expenditure on necessities? This segment of your financial Plan should be supported by guaranteed income streams such as Social Security, pensions, and other forms of protected lifetime income.

Variable Spending Essential Question - How much does your spending fluctuate each month? Earnings from dividend-paying stocks and funds, fixed-income securities, and cash or cash equivalents can cover this.

Legacy Spending Essential Question - What are your intentions and plans for your estate and heirs? Allocations for this should include growth-oriented portfolios and alternative capital preservation strategies.

Understanding your stable versus variable spending requirements is crucial before developing a diversified and growth-oriented strategy. A sophisticated growth-focused portfolio may not be necessary if your goal is to ensure a steady income stream. When considering the development of an investment portfolio, it's vital to explore and understand target-date funds. These funds are specifically designed for retirement planning and adjust their investment mix as your retirement date approaches.

This shift towards more conservative investments as you near retirement reduces risk. Target-date funds provide a simplified investment approach, ideal for those who prefer a more hands-off strategy. However, it's essential to be aware of their fees and the asset allocation strategy they employ.

Inflation is an often-overlooked risk to your savings, gradually diminishing your purchasing power. To safeguard against this, consider incorporating inflation-protected securities into your portfolio, such as Treasury Inflation-Protected Securities (TIPS), designed to adjust with Inflation. Adapting your investment strategy to include protections against Inflation, such as maintaining a portion of your portfolio in stocks, is advisable. Stocks have historically outperformed Inflation over time. It's important to regularly review your investment mix to ensure it remains in line with your risk tolerance and inflationary expectations.

It's clear from this discussion that investment strategies are not universal; what works for one may not suit another. There's little benefit in pursuing a complex investment strategy geared towards growth if your financial needs don't align with such an approach. The initial step involves thoroughly assessing your stable versus variable spending requirements for retirement. This critical analysis paves the way to determine whether a more diversified and growth-focused investment strategy suits you.

Suppose you are looking to develop an Investment Portfolio. In that case, it will be critical for you to research and consider Target-date funds. They are another tool tailored for retirement needs. These funds adjust their investment mix based on your retirement timeline. As you get closer to retirement, they shift to more conservative investments. This reduces risk as you near the time when you will need to draw on your savings. They offer a hands-off approach, which can be beneficial if you prefer to avoid managing investments actively. However, it's essential to understand their fees and their specific asset allocation strategy.

6.5 PRODUCT INTEGRATION TO HELP FUND VARIABLE EXPENSES

Understanding the Risks and Benefits of Mutual Funds

Mutual funds operate on a collective investment scheme, pooling money from multiple investors to purchase a diversified portfolio of stocks, bonds, or other securities. Managed by professionals, these funds aim to spread risk and offer investors access to a wider array of investments than they might manage individually, making it an attractive option for those intimidated by handling stocks directly. The primary advantage of mutual funds is diversification, reducing the risk of significant financial loss by spreading investments across various assets. Professional management relieves investors of the burden of making complex investment decisions, a boon for retirees seeking a simpler way to preserve and grow their wealth without diving deep into market analysis. However, mutual funds are not without risks. Market volatility can affect the fund's value, and management fees can diminish returns. These fees vary among funds, emphasizing the importance of understanding and comparing costs against potential gains. When selecting a mutual fund, align the fund's objectives with your personal investment goals, whether seeking growth, income, or a combination. Evaluate the fund's performance history, management style, and risk tolerance to ensure it fits your investment strategy. This thoughtful approach helps in choosing a mutual fund that complements your retirement planning effectively.

Consider Louisa, who wanted her investments to support her retirement while aligning with her values. She chose a socially responsible mutual fund. This fund aims to achieve financial returns and focuses on companies with strong environmental and social records. Louisa appreciated that the fund's goals matched her own, and she felt more confident knowing her money supported causes she cared about. The fund had a strong performance history with a management style she found appealing. Louisa's choice illustrates how aligning personal values with investment strategies can enhance satisfaction and confidence in your financial decisions.

Exploring the Reverse Mortgage Option

A reverse mortgage offers homeowners aged 62 and older a way to convert part of their home equity into cash without the need for monthly loan repayments. This financial tool becomes repayable upon the sale of the home, the homeowner moving out permanently, or their passing. Eligibility hinges on owning your home outright or having a minimal mortgage balance that the reverse mortgage can settle. The borrowing amount is influenced by the homeowner's age, the property's value, and prevailing interest rates, with older individuals and more valuable homes qualifying for larger sums. The primary advantage of a reverse mortgage is the provision of a steady income stream for retirees to cover living expenses, medical bills, or home improvements while retaining home ownership. Yet, it's important to note the drawbacks: the loan balance increases over time due to accumulating interest, potentially diminishing home equity and affecting inheritance plans. Homeowners must also continue to pay property taxes, insurance, and maintain their property to avoid foreclosure. Before deciding on a reverse mortgage, consider your long-term housing intentions and future financial needs, especially if planning to leave your home to heirs, as it might reduce the inheritance value. Discussing potential impacts with your family and carefully assessing your financial situation are crucial steps in determining if a reverse mortgage aligns with your retirement goals.Let's consider a few real-life scenarios.

We will now explore how to plan your legacy, ensuring that your hard-earned wealth will support you and your loved ones in years to come.

6.6: ESTATE PLANNING AND LEGACY EXPENSES

Imagine this: you've spent years building a life and accumulating assets, yet without a plan, the future of those assets remains uncertain. This is where estate planning steps in. It ensures that your wishes are honoured after you pass away. A will is one of the most critical tools in this process. Rather than leaving it to the state, it lets you decide who gets what. Without a will, your assets might be distributed according to laws that don't reflect your wishes. You can designate beneficiaries, ensuring your hard-earned assets go to the people or organizations you care about. This can prevent disputes among family members, making a difficult time a little easier. If you have minor children, a will allows you to appoint guardians. This decision ensures that they are cared for by someone you trust.

Trusts provide another layer of control and flexibility in estate planning. Unlike a will, which goes into effect after death, a trust can manage your assets during your lifetime. This can be particularly useful if you become unable to handle your affairs. Trusts can also help avoid probate, the legal process of distributing your estate. Probate can be lengthy and costly, but a living trust allows for swift asset distribution. This privacy can be invaluable, allowing for a discreet transfer of assets. There are different types of trusts, including revocable and irrevocable trusts. You can change or end a revocable trust at any time. This flexibility is useful if your circumstances change. An irrevocable trust, however, cannot be altered once established. It provides stronger protection against taxes and creditors.

Drafting wills and trusts requires careful thought and professional guidance. Consulting with an estate attorney ensures your documents meet legal standards and accurately reflect your desires. An attorney can guide you through the complexities of estate laws and help tailor your Plan to your specific needs. It's crucial to regularly update these documents to reflect any life changes. This includes changes in marital status, the birth of a child, or the acquisition of significant assets. Keeping your estate plan current prevents confusion and ensures it aligns with your situation. It's also important to consider digital assets, such as online accounts and digital currencies. It is important to account for these to ensure them are protected and secured.

There are common mistakes in estate planning that you should avoid. One major pitfall is not planning for incapacity. This oversight can leave your affairs in disarray if you cannot make decisions. Establishing powers of attorney and healthcare directives can address this issue, allowing someone you trust to make decisions on your behalf. Another common mistake is overlooking digital assets. These assets hold significant value in today's digital age, yet many people neglect to include them in their estate plans. To avoid this, list all online accounts and digital assets. Provide clear instructions on how they should be handled. This foresight can ensure these assets are managed according to your wishes.

Resource List: Estate Planning Essentials

- Consult an Estate Attorney: Seek professional advice to ensure your documents are legally sound and reflect your wishes.
- Review and Update Regularly: Revisit your estate plan every few years or after major life events to keep it relevant.

- Include Digital Assets: List all online accounts and provide access instructions to protect them.
- Appoint Powers of Attorney: Designate trusted individuals to make decisions if you become incapacitated.

These steps are crucial in creating a comprehensive estate plan that safeguards your legacy and provides peace of mind.

Protecting Your Assets and Heirs

Safeguarding your wealth for future generations involves a mix of strategies. Asset protection trusts provide a legal barrier, shielding your assets from potential threats like creditors and lawsuits. Insurance policies also serve as a financial safety net, covering liabilities that could diminish your estate. By combining these tools, you create a robust defence against unforeseen challenges.

Beneficiary designations are crucial - they determine who receives benefits from accounts like retirement funds and life insurance. Regularly reviewing and updating these records ensures your assets go to the right people, avoiding family disputes.

Minimizing estate taxes is another key consideration. Strategic gifting, such as annual cash contributions to family members, can lower your taxable estate. Establishing charitable remainder trusts is another effective approach, providing income to beneficiaries while directing the remainder to causes you care about.

Legal structures like family limited partnerships (FLPs) offer protection and tax benefits. FLPs allow you to transfer assets to family at a discount, reducing estate taxes while retaining control over how assets are used and distributed.

By incorporating these strategies, you protect your assets and secure your heirs' future. Each method offers unique advantages that can be tailored to your circumstances, ensuring your legacy endures and reflects your values.

Planning Your Legacy: More Than Just Money

When considering your legacy, think beyond money and possessions. A legacy includes the values and principles you pass on to your heirs. These elements can shape how your family remembers you and how they choose to live their lives. It's about instilling values that matter to you, such as honesty, perseverance, or kindness. Creating a family mission statement can help articulate these ideals. This statement reflects what you stand for and the principles you hope your family will uphold. It can guide decisions and serve as a moral compass for future generations. Doing this ensures that your legacy includes more than material wealth—it embodies the essence of who you are.

Your estate plan should reflect your personal beliefs and values. This can be achieved by establishing educational trusts for future generations. Such trusts provide funds for education, helping your children or grandchildren achieve their academic goals. They can also include stipulations that align with your values, such as maintaining a certain grade point average or volunteering in the community. This approach supports their education and encourages personal growth and responsibility. By tying financial support to values, you reinforce the importance of these principles in their lives. This thoughtful planning ensures your legacy continues to influence and inspire even after you're gone.

Philanthropic endeavours can also play a big role in your legacy. Charitable giving allows you to support causes that matter to you, creating a lasting impact. One way to do this is by creating donor-advised funds. These funds let you donate to charities over time while receiving immediate tax benefits. They offer flexibility in choosing which charities to support and when. Another option is setting up a family foundation. This allows your family to work together on charitable projects, fostering unity and shared purpose. Involving family in these decisions can teach them the value of giving and stewardship. These acts of generosity extend your influence and reflect your values on a larger scale.

Reflecting on your legacy goals requires introspection. Engage in reflective journaling to clarify your intentions. Ask yourself what you hope to leave behind. Consider what makes you proud and what you want your family to remember. Please write down your thoughts and revisit them regularly. This practice helps crystallize your vision and ensures your legacy aligns with your deepest values. It can reveal insights into how you wish to be remembered and what impact you hope to have. By understanding these desires, you can create an estate plan reflecting your legacy's broader impact. This reflection is about financial planning and crafting a narrative that speaks to your life's purpose and the values you hold dear.

Navigating Family Dynamics in Estate Decisions

Family dynamics can significantly impact estate planning. If not addressed, differing expectations, such as assumptions about inheriting the family home, can lead to conflicts. Blended families face additional challenges, requiring sensitivity in balancing the needs of a new spouse and children from a previous marriage.

Facilitating open family discussions is crucial. These meetings provide a space to share your intentions and listen to concerns, helping align expectations. Explaining the reasoning behind your decisions promotes understanding, even if everyone doesn't agree.

When disputes arise, engaging a neutral mediator can help resolve contentious issues. They offer an unbiased perspective to ease tensions and foster cooperation, leading to solutions that satisfy all parties.

Transparency and fairness are key. Documenting your choices and sharing them with your family ensures everyone understands the Plan, manages expectations, and reduces the risk of surprises. Fairness involves considering each individual's needs, not necessarily equal shares.

By navigating these family dynamics through open communication, mediation, and balanced decision-making, you can create an estate plan that protects your assets while strengthening family bonds and ensuring your legacy reflects your values.

CHAPTER 7
STEP 6: HOLISTIC RETIREMENT PLANNING - BEYOND FINANCIAL, THE EMOTIONAL AND SOCIAL SIDES OF RETIREMENT

"Preparation for old age should begin not later than one's teens. A life which is empty of purpose until 65 will not suddenly become filled on retirement."

ARTHUR E. MORGAN

7.1 PROACTIVELY ADDRESSING HEALTH AND WELLNESS

Maintaining health is paramount as you enter retirement, with good health enhancing life quality and reducing healthcare costs. Exercise is crucial; aim for 150 minutes of moderate activities like walking, swimming, or yoga weekly. These low-impact exercises are ideal for older adults, promoting flexibility and muscle strength, heart health, and mood. Nutrition is equally important. A balanced diet rich in vitamins, minerals, and fiber from fruits, vegetables, whole grains, and lean proteins fuels your body and supports longevity. Limit intake of processed foods and stay hydrated to aid in digestion and keep your body functioning optimally. Mental health should not be overlooked. Retirement's changes may affect emotional well-being, making access to counseling and support groups valuable. Engage in mental wellness activities like meditation or journaling and keep your mind active with hobbies or learning new skills to maintain cognitive health. Preventive health measures, including regular check-ups, screenings, and staying current with vaccinations, are essential to catch health issues early and stay healthy. A simple wellness checklist can guide daily habits for maintaining health: practice good hygiene, balance your diet, stay hydrated, maintain a regular sleep schedule of seven to nine hours, engage in social activities, and practice relaxation techniques to reduce stress. Small steps in maintaining health lead to significant benefits, allowing you to enjoy a fulfilling and vibrant retirement. Prioritizing your health enables you to pursue interests and maximize your retirement years, ensuring you remain vibrant and enjoy all that retirement has to offer.

7.2 EMOTIONAL AND SOCIAL WELL-BEING IN RETIREMENT

Imagine waking up on the first day of your retirement with no pressing tasks, free from the stress of daily work responsibilities. For some, this newfound freedom feels liberating. But for others, it can bring unexpected challenges. The transition from a structured work environment to a more open-ended lifestyle can be difficult. Many retirees struggle with a loss of identity after leaving a long-term career. Work often provides a sense of purpose and belonging. Without it, you might feel adrift and uncertain about your place in the world. This chapter will explore how to rediscover your sense of purpose, helping you forge a fulfilling life beyond your career.

The end of a career often means the end of a routine that structured your days and defined your role in society. This shift can lead to feelings of loss and anxiety. Many retirees experience a decline in mental health, including increased stress and depression, as they adjust to their new reality. It can be challenging to fill the void left by work. However, this stage of life also presents an opportunity to explore new interests and passions. The key is to embrace change and view it as a chance to redefine yourself.

Finding new passions can transform your retirement experience. Consider volunteering in your community, which fills your time and provides a sense of purpose and connection. Explore activities that interest you, whether helping at a local animal shelter or mentoring young professionals. Creative pursuits like painting, writing, or playing an instrument can also offer fulfilment. These activities stimulate your mind and add joy to your days. They encourage you to discover talents and interests you may have overlooked during your working years. Engaging in such activities creates a new identity that reflects your values and interests.

Building and Nurturing Social Networks

As you enter retirement, maintaining and building social connections becomes vital for your emotional well-being. Relationships play a key role in supporting mental health and happiness. They provide comfort, reduce stress, and enhance your quality of life. Without the daily interactions that work provides, it is easy to feel disconnected. However, retirement offers an excellent opportunity to expand your social circles and create new friendships. By actively seeking social opportunities, you can fill your days with meaningful interactions that enrich your life. These connections also serve as a support system, helping you navigate the changes with retirement.

One way to meet new people is by joining local clubs or community groups. These organizations often welcome new members with open arms. Consider joining a book club, gardening group, or sports team that matches your interests. These gatherings provide a relaxed setting to meet like-minded individuals. Another option is attending social events or classes offered in your community. Libraries, community centres, and senior centres often host events that bring people together. These activities introduce you to new faces and keep your mind active and engaged. Participating in these groups allows you to build a network of friends who share your interests.

Technology plays a crucial role in staying connected with friends and family, especially those who live far away. Social media platforms offer an easy way to reconnect with old friends and forge new relationships. They allow you to share updates and photos, keeping your loved ones close even when miles apart. Video calls also offer a personal touch, allowing you to see the faces of those you care about. Apps like Skype or Zoom make it simple to chat with family members or friends anytime. These digital tools help bridge the distance, making it possible to maintain strong connections despite physical separation.

Nurturing existing relationships is just as important as forming new ones. Simple actions like regular meet-ups or phone calls can strengthen bonds. Make an effort to reach out to friends and family regularly. Set a consistent schedule for calls or visits, ensuring you stay in touch. Sharing meals or engaging in shared activities can deepen connections. These interactions provide a chance to create new memories and reinforce the ties that bind you. Showing appreciation and gratitude also strengthens relationships. Taking the time to express your feelings can enhance mutual respect and affection. These efforts ensure your relationships remain strong and supportive throughout retirement.

Building and maintaining social networks require intention and effort, but the rewards are immense. Strong social ties contribute to a more fulfilling and enjoyable retirement. They offer companionship, support, and joy. They help prevent loneliness and isolation, which can negatively impact health. You create a vibrant and connected life by actively engaging in social activities. This engagement enriches your retirement years, providing a sense of belonging and community. Your relationships become a cornerstone of your well-being, offering stability and happiness as you embrace this new chapter.

Combating Loneliness and Social Isolation

The transition into retirement is an exciting time for many, but it can also bring unexpected feelings of loneliness. This loneliness often stems from several factors. Many people lose the daily social interactions that work provides. Without these, they may feel isolated. Another cause is the physical distance from family or friends who might have moved away. Losing a spouse or close friend can also deepen feelings of isolation. Recognizing these risk factors is the first step in addressing them. Signs of loneliness include:

- Feelings of sadness.
- A lack of motivation to engage in activities.
- A sense of disconnection from others.

If you experience these feelings, remember that you are not alone and that there are ways to reconnect and thrive.

Reducing loneliness involves taking practical steps to increase social engagement. One effective way to combat isolation is participating in group activities or clubs. These provide a sense of belonging and purpose. Whether joining a local history club, a walking group, or a sports team, these activities offer regular opportunities to meet others. They also encourage you to step out of your comfort zone and engage with people who share similar interests. Another option is to seek out neighbourhood events. Many communities host regular gatherings like farmers' markets, festivals, or charity events. These occasions are perfect for mingling and meeting new people in a relaxed setting. Attending these events can help you feel more connected to your local community.

Pets can also play a significant role in reducing loneliness. Adopting a pet can provide companionship and routine. Pets offer unconditional love and comfort, which can be especially beneficial during times of change. They encourage physical activity and regular schedules, such as daily walks or feeding times. This structure can be comforting and provide a sense of purpose. Dogs, cats, and smaller animals like birds or rabbits can bring joy and companionship. Caring for a pet can also connect you with other pet owners through local parks or online communities. These connections can lead to new friendships and shared experiences. The presence of a pet can brighten your days and give you a sense of fulfillment.

Professional support is available for those who continue to struggle with isolation. Local support groups or helplines offer guidance and companionship. These resources provide a safe space to share feelings and experiences with others who understand. Support groups often meet regularly, offering both social interaction and emotional support. Helplines can be a valuable resource for immediate assistance or advice. They connect you with trained counsellors who can guide your situation. Seeking help is a sign of strength, not weakness, and can be an essential step in overcoming loneliness. Remember, it's okay to reach out for support when needed.

Resource List: Support for Combating Loneliness

- Local Support Groups: Check community centres or libraries for listings of local groups focused on social interaction and support.
- Helplines: Consider national helplines like the Friendship Line at 1-800-971-0016, which offers advice and companionship for older adults.
- Online Resources: Websites like MeetUp.com can help you find local groups and activities that match your interests.

These resources can offer a lifeline, providing practical advice and emotional support. They remind you that help is out there and you don't have to face loneliness alone. You can create a fulfilling retirement filled with connections and joy by taking active steps to engage with others, adopt a pet, or seek professional support.

7.3 ENGAGING IN COMMUNITY AND VOLUNTEER WORK

Participating in community activities and volunteering can greatly enhance your retirement, adding a profound sense of purpose and joy. Engaging in such meaningful activities not only benefits those around you but also boosts your mental health, reducing depression and anxiety. To find the right volunteer opportunity, start by reflecting on your skills and interests, then explore local non-profits and charities or use websites like volunteermatch.org to find matches. Volunteering is not just about giving; it's a mutual exchange that enriches your life and builds connections. Group volunteering, in particular, offers a unique way to forge friendships and a sense of community, making your retirement more satisfying and connected.

Consider the story of Mary, a retiree who found a new purpose through volunteering. After retiring from a long career in education, Mary felt disconnected from her community. She began volunteering at a local literacy centre, helping adults improve their reading skills. This role allowed her to use her teaching skills in a new way, providing her with a sense of fulfillment and pride. She met other volunteers who shared her passion for education through this work. Together, they formed a tight-knit group, supporting each other in their mission to make a difference. Mary's story shows how volunteering can transform your retirement, providing both personal satisfaction and meaningful connections.

Another inspiring example is Tom, who spent his career as an engineer. In retirement, he sought ways to apply his technical skills to benefit his community. He joined a non-profit that focused on building sustainable housing for low-income families. Tom found great joy in using his expertise to help those in need. The project teams he worked with became like a second family. They shared meals, celebrated successes, and supported each other during challenges. Tom's involvement not only improved the lives of others but also enriched his own, showing that community work offers rewards beyond the tangible.

Engaging in community and volunteer work allows you to remain active and connected, providing a sense of purpose and fulfillment that enriches your retirement life.

As you consider your next steps in retirement, exploring different types of retirement communities might appeal to you. Independent communities offer a lifestyle where you maintain autonomy while still having access to shared amenities and social opportunities. These communities often resemble small neighbourhoods or apartment complexes. They provide a setting to enjoy your day without home maintenance responsibilities. Here, you can participate in various activities or enjoy the peace of your space. It's a perfect blend of independence and community support, allowing you to live on your terms.

Continuing Care Retirement Communities, or CCRCs, are another option. They cater to varying levels of care needs. Starting with independent living, they offer assisted living and skilled nursing care as needed. This setup provides a sense of security, knowing you won't need to move should your health needs change. It's an all-in-one approach, where you can stay in the same community and receive the appropriate level of care over time. CCRCs are ideal if you're looking for a long-term living arrangement with the flexibility to adapt as your health needs evolve.

Assisted living facilities cater to those who require more daily assistance. These facilities help with everyday tasks such as bathing, dressing, and medication management. The environment supports independence while ensuring that help is readily available. Assisted living offers a balance of personal care and social interaction, with staff available to meet your needs around the clock. This option is well-suited if you or a loved one require more personalized care but still wish to maintain independence.

When evaluating retirement communities, the amenities and services available can significantly impact your decision. On-site healthcare services and wellness programs are vital. Having access to medical care without leaving the community ensures peace of mind. Look for communities that offer regular health check-ups, therapy services, and emergency response systems. Social and recreational facilities also play a crucial role. Check for fitness centres, swimming pools, and organized activities. These features enhance your lifestyle and provide opportunities for engagement and friendship. The right amenities can make a significant difference in your quality of life.

Financial considerations are crucial when choosing a retirement community. Many communities require entrance fees, which are upfront costs that secure your place and sometimes contribute to long-term care funds. Monthly service charges cover daily living expenses, including utilities, meals, and activities. Understanding contract types and refund policies is also essential. Some contracts offer a return on your entrance fee if you leave, while others do not. Make sure to read the fine print and ask questions about what's included and what's not. This knowledge helps you assess whether a community fits within your budget.

When you tour potential communities, having a checklist can be invaluable. Important questions include: What healthcare services are offered, and how are they staffed? Are there any additional fees for using specific amenities? What social activities are available, and how often do they occur? Understanding the community's policies on visitors, pets, and transportation can also be helpful. Consider speaking with current residents to get their perspectives. Their insights can provide a real-world understanding of daily life in the community. Armed with this information, you can make an informed decision that aligns with your lifestyle and needs.

7.4 CULTIVATING HOBBIES AND LIFELONG LEARNING

Engaging in hobbies is not merely a pastime; it plays a crucial role in keeping your mind active and sharp. In retirement, when the regular demands of a job subside, hobbies offer a way to stay mentally stimulated. They challenge your brain in new ways, which is vital for maintaining cognitive health. Activities like puzzles or strategy games can provide this mental workout. These games require focus and problem-solving, which help keep your brain engaged. Hobbies also offer a sense of accomplishment, which is important for emotional well-being. Whether it's completing a challenging puzzle or learning the nuances of a new game, these activities provide satisfaction and joy. They offer a break from routine, introducing novelty and excitement into your daily life.

Exploring new hobbies can open doors to experiences you never thought possible. Retirement is an ideal time to try diverse activities. Consider joining a book club or a writing group. These gatherings stimulate your mind and offer social interaction. They provide opportunities to share ideas and learn from others. Art or craft workshops appeal if you enjoy working with your hands. These settings allow you to express creativity and learn new skills. They also offer a space to connect with others who share your interests. Trying new hobbies can broaden your horizons and introduce you to new communities. This exploration enriches your life, adding layers of meaning and purpose.

Lifelong learning is another powerful tool to enhance your retirement. Education doesn't have to end when you retire. It can be an exciting and fulfilling part of your later years. Learning new things provides challenges and keeps you curious. Whether you enrol in local college classes or explore online courses, education offers endless possibilities. Many institutions offer programs specifically designed for older adults. These classes are often more flexible and less formal, making them perfect for retirees. They cover many subjects, from history to technology, providing plenty of options to pique your interest. The pursuit of knowledge keeps your mind active and your outlook fresh.

Accessing educational opportunities has never been easier, thanks to the internet. Websites like Coursera or Khan Academy offer numerous free online courses. These platforms allow you to learn at your own pace, covering exciting subjects. You can join discussions, complete assignments, and gain new insights from the comfort of your home. Local community colleges also offer programs tailored to older adults. These classes can be a great way to dive into a subject you've always wanted to explore. They also provide a structured learning environment, which can be motivating and rewarding. Engaging in education opens your world, connecting you to new ideas and people.

As you explore hobbies and learning, remember to enjoy the process. These activities should bring joy and satisfaction, enhancing your retirement experience. They provide structure and purpose, filling your days with meaning. They challenge your mind, keeping it sharp and engaged. They also introduce you to new communities, broadening your social network. By incorporating hobbies and learning into your routine, you enrich your life. This enrichment supports your overall well-being, making retirement a time of growth and discovery.

With hobbies and lifelong learning enriching your days, you set the stage for a fulfilling retirement. These pursuits offer more than just a way to pass the time. They keep you mentally active, socially connected, and emotionally satisfied. As you continue to explore new interests and learn new things, you create a vibrant and engaging life. This vibrancy ensures that your retirement years are some of the most rewarding.

7.5 HOUSING AND RELOCATION DECISIONS

Imagine standing in your living room, surrounded by memories—photos of family gatherings, that favourite chair by the window, the creaky floorboard that always announces your arrival. Downsizing means leaving behind more than just square footage. It involves parting with a home full of memories. For many, the thought of moving into a smaller space is daunting. According to a recent study, 51% of seniors who have moved chose to downsize. The decision to leave a long-term home is not just about practicality; it is deeply emotional. The memories and personal history tied to your home can overwhelm the process. Each room holds stories and moments that you cherish. Parting with these can feel like losing a part of yourself.

The psychological challenges of downsizing often stem from attachment. You may find it hard to let go of sentimental belongings. Each item has a story, a connection to a time or person you hold dear. The fear of the unknown can also weigh heavily. Moving to a new place means adapting to a different environment. It requires letting go of the familiar comforts of your current home. This transition can lead to stress and anxiety as you leave behind the security of what you know. To address these feelings, it helps to acknowledge and celebrate the memories your home holds. Take time to reflect on the good times and the life you built there. This can provide a sense of closure and readiness to move forward.

One effective strategy for managing the emotional impact of downsizing is to start with less emotionally significant areas. Begin decluttering in rooms like the bathroom or kitchen, where items may carry less sentimental weight. Sorting possessions into categories can help simplify the process. Decide which items to sell, donate, recycle, or keep. The Kondo Method, made popular by

Marie Kondo, suggests keeping only those items that "spark joy." This approach encourages you to focus on what truly matters and let go of the rest. Consider organizing a garage sale or donation drive for items that no longer serve you. Not only does this clear space, it also allows others to benefit from things you no longer need.

Transitioning to a smaller space requires thoughtful planning. Designing multi-functional spaces helps maximize your new environment. Consider furniture that serves dual purposes, like a sofa bed or a dining table that doubles as a workspace. Prioritizing comfort and accessibility is essential. Ensure your new home is easy to navigate and meets your needs. This might mean choosing a single-story layout or installing grab bars for safety. These adjustments can make your new space feel welcoming and practical. It's essential to create a living area that feels like home. Incorporating familiar items, like a favourite chair or cherished photos, can bring comfort and continuity to the new space.

The journey of downsizing is often filled with lessons and inspiration. Take the example of Harold and June, a couple who decided to downsize after retirement. They approached the process with a clear plan and enlisted help from family to sort through decades of belongings. They found freedom in their new, smaller home by focusing on what brought them joy and letting go of the rest. They designed their space with multi-functional furniture, creating a cozy and efficient living environment. Their story is a testament to the positive outcomes of downsizing. It highlights the opportunity to reinvent one's lifestyle and reduce responsibilities, paving the way for a fresh start and new adventures.

Interactive Exercise: Preparing for Your Move

Consider these questions as you prepare for downsizing:

- What items in your home hold the most sentimental value?
- How can you incorporate these cherished belongings into your new space?
- What aspects of your current home do you want to replicate in your new home?
- How can family or friends support you during this transition?

Reflecting on these questions can help ease the emotional transition. It can also help you plan a move that honors your past while embracing the future. As you embark on this new chapter, remember that downsizing is an opportunity to create a space that truly reflects your current needs and aspirations.

Implications of Moving in Retirement

Relocating in retirement offers the excitement of new beginnings and potentially lower living costs but comes with substantial financial considerations. Selling a home incurs costs such as agent commissions, typically 5-6% of the sale price, and closing costs, which can diminish profits. Additionally, buying a new home introduces expenses like mortgage application fees and appraisal costs. It's crucial to budget for these and consider potential taxes, such as capital gains from selling your property or transfer taxes when buying. The cost of living in a new area can significantly impact your retirement budget, potentially introducing higher expenses in sectors like healthcare or groceries, even if housing is cheaper. It's essential to research and compare costs to ensure relocating aligns with your financial goals, maintaining a balanced and sustainable budget. Timing also plays a critical role in the financial outcome of selling and buying properties. Market trends can influence the best times to sell or buy, with spring and early summer often being more advantageous for sellers, and late fall or winter potentially benefiting buyers. Consulting a real estate professional can provide valuable insights into local market conditions and help navigate these decisions. Considering alternative housing arrangements, such as co-housing communities or renting, can provide different financial and lifestyle benefits. Co-housing can reduce living costs and offer a sense of community, while renting allows for flexibility and avoids the long-term financial commitments of homeownership. Each option requires weighing the pros and cons, considering personal space, freedom to move, and investment potential. Consulting with a financial advisor can offer personalized guidance, helping evaluate how different housing options fit into your overall retirement plan. Making informed decisions about housing in retirement is crucial for enhancing both financial security and personal fulfillment.

Adapting Your Home for Aging in Place

Imagine waking up each day in the comfort of your own home, surrounded by familiar sights and sounds. This is the essence of aging in place. It's about staying in the environment you know and love while making it safe and accessible. Many people prefer this option because it allows them to maintain their independence. You avoid the emotional and physical stress of moving to a new place. Your home holds memories, and staying there can provide a sense of continuity and stability. Aging in place lets you control your living situation, making it a popular choice for many as they grow older.

Consider some practical modifications to make your home safe and functional for aging in place. Start with installing grab bars and railings in bathrooms and hallways. These additions can prevent falls and provide support. Another critical change is creating step-free access to living areas. This might mean adding ramps or removing rugs that could cause trips. Look at your home's layout. Ensure essential spaces, like the bathroom and kitchen, are easily accessible. These changes may seem small, but they can make a big difference in your daily life. They help you move around your home with ease and confidence.

Technology offers exciting solutions to enhance safety and comfort at home. Smart home devices can be your allies in maintaining independence. Consider installing smart doorbells and security systems. These allow you to see who is at your door without getting up. Smart thermostats and lighting control systems can also add convenience. You can adjust the temperature or lights with a simple voice command or tap on your phone. Emergency alert systems are another valuable tool. They can notify family or medical services if you need help. Knowing you have support at your fingertips, these technologies provide peace of mind.

Finding the right professionals to help with home modifications is crucial. You want experts who understand your needs and can deliver quality work. Start by reaching out to local aging-in-place specialists. They are trained to assess homes and recommend necessary changes. Look for contractors who have experience with senior home renovations. Check their credentials and ask for references. This will help ensure they have done similar work before. Some communities have resources to connect you with reliable professionals. It might be worth consulting local agencies or online directories for recommendations. Engaging the right people ensures your home is safe and comfortable as you age.

7.6 PURSUING ENCORE CAREERS AND PASSION PROJECTS

Stepping into retirement opens doors to encore careers, transforming old skills into new opportunities. This phase allows you to explore long-held passions, perhaps turning a hobby into a career that feels more like joy than work. For example, an accountant might pivot to teaching financial literacy, while a healthcare professional could consult for wellness programs. Embracing what you love can lead to launching a small business, creating a blog, or starting community initiatives that align with your interests, such as sustainable gardening or crafting. These activities not only fulfill personal passions but also contribute to your community, offering social engagement and intellectual stimulation. They help avoid the isolation some retirees experience, keeping the mind sharp and providing a sense of purpose. Moreover, they can offer additional income, easing the financial transition into retirement and affording more luxuries or family support. Many retirees find success and satisfaction in such endeavors. A former teacher might start a community art program, using their skills to inspire creativity in others. An engineer could establish a business focused on sustainable practices, combining technical expertise with environmental passion. These examples highlight the potential for a fulfilling retirement through pursuing personal interests and engaging in meaningful work.

Interactive Element: Identifying Your Passion Project

Here is a simple exercise to help you identify a passion project:

- Reflect on Interests: What hobbies or activities bring you joy? List them out.
- Assess Skills: What skills have you gained over your career? Consider how they might apply to a new project.

- Explore Opportunities: Research community needs or market gaps where your interests and skills might fit.
- Set Goals: Define what success looks like for your project. This could be financial, personal satisfaction, or community impact.
- Take Action: Start small. Take the first step towards your passion project and see where it leads you.

This exercise helps you focus on what you love and how to make it a meaningful part of your retirement.

CHAPTER 8
MANAGING COMMON RETIREMENT CHALLENGES

"Our very survival depends on our ability to stay awake, to adjust to new ideas, to remain vigilant and to face the challenge of change."

MARTIN LUTHER KING JR.

Imagine sitting at your dining table, balancing your chequebook while your grandchild tugs at your sleeve, asking for help with college fees. It's a scene many retirees know too well. Many feel a strong urge to support their children and grandchildren financially, even when it affects their own retirement savings. You have worked hard to build a nest egg, but emotional ties can make it hard to say no. Supporting family members often means dipping into savings intended for your future needs. This generosity can quickly lead to financial strain if not managed well. It's important to recognize the impact on your retirement savings and the potential for your funds to dwindle faster than planned. This is a common challenge, and addressing it requires a balance between helping loved ones and maintaining your financial security.

Establishing boundaries around financial support is key. This does not mean you cannot help your family. It means setting limits that protect your financial well-being while allowing you to assist where possible. Start by assessing your financial situation. Determine what you can afford to give without compromising your own needs. Consider creating a separate budget for family assistance. This keeps your own expenses and savings on track. Clear boundaries prevent misunderstandings and help maintain healthy relationships. You can offer support without risking your financial future. These boundaries help you manage expectations, both yours and theirs. It ensures that your generosity doesn't jeopardize your retirement goals.

Maintaining personal financial security while helping family is possible with careful planning. Define your financial goals and limits clearly. Know what you want to achieve for yourself in retirement. This might include travel plans, healthcare needs, or pursuing hobbies. A clear picture of your financial priorities guides your decisions about family support. It helps you stay focused on your own needs. When you decide to help, consider the form it takes. Instead of giving cash, offer to pay for specific services like education or healthcare. This provides support while keeping control over how your money is used. It aligns with your budget and goals, ensuring your generosity is sustainable.

Open communication with family about financial matters is crucial. Discuss expectations and limitations openly. Family meetings can provide a platform for these conversations. Use this time to explain your financial plan and the role family support plays in it. Encourage family members to share their needs and expectations as well. Transparency helps avoid assumptions and misunderstandings. It builds trust and strengthens relationships. Consider using tools like family financial agreements. These documents outline agreed-upon terms and expectations. They provide clarity and serve as a reference if questions arise later. Clear communication and agreements protect your financial interests and family harmony.

8.1 STAYING UPDATED ON FINANCIAL LAWS AND OPPORTUNITIES

The world of finance is constantly changing. New laws and opportunities arise, affecting how you should plan for retirement. Staying informed about these changes is crucial for making the best decisions. For example, recent changes in tax laws can impact how much you save or withdraw. Knowing these updates helps you adjust your strategy and maximize your savings. Tax laws don't just change the rates; they can alter deductions and credits, which affect your overall tax bill. Retirement account regulations can also shift. New rules might change how you contribute or when you must take distributions. Understanding these changes means you can avoid penalties and leverage new benefits.

Accessing reliable financial information is critical to staying informed. One effective way is by subscribing to financial newsletters. These newsletters can provide regular updates about changes in laws and regulations. They break down complex information into simple terms, making it accessible. Another option is attending seminars and workshops on retirement planning. These events offer insights from experts who explain the implications of recent changes. They also provide a platform to ask questions and clarify doubts. You can take advantage of new opportunities by staying engaged with these resources. This proactive approach ensures that you are always prepared, no matter how the financial landscape shifts.

When new opportunities arise, it's essential to incorporate them into your plans. Adjusting your investment portfolio is one way to do this. New tax incentives make certain investments more attractive. For example, changes in capital gains tax rates could influence your decision to sell or hold stocks. By aligning your portfolio with these incentives, you can enhance your returns. Being flexible and ready to adapt helps you stay ahead. It's about recognizing when to pivot and making informed decisions that benefit your financial health. This might mean reallocating assets or exploring new investment vehicles. The key is to remain open to change and willing to adjust your plans.

Consider the story of Mark, a retiree who used updated laws to improve his financial situation. Mark learned about changes in the tax code that affected retirement account distributions. By attending a local workshop, he discovered a strategy for tax-efficient withdrawals. This involved taking distributions from his Roth IRA, which were tax-free, and delaying withdrawals from his traditional IRA. This approach reduced his taxable income and minimized his tax burden. As a result, Mark could maintain a higher standard of living without depleting his savings. His experience shows the benefits of staying informed and adapting to new regulations. It highlights how leveraging current laws can lead to smarter financial decisions.

Engaging with these resources and strategies helps you navigate the complexities of retirement planning. It ensures you can maximise your savings and investments, providing a secure foundation for your future. By staying up-to-date with financial changes, you protect your interests and seize opportunities that align with your goals. This vigilance not only safeguards your current assets but also opens doors to new avenues of growth and security. Being proactive and informed empowers you to steer your retirement in the right direction, adapting to whatever changes come your way.

8.2 MANAGING THE EMOTIONAL IMPACT OF RETIREMENT TRANSITIONS

Retirement can feel like standing at the edge of a new world. The routine you've followed for decades suddenly changes. With this shift, many retirees face emotional challenges. You might feel a loss of identity and structure. Work often gives us purpose and a sense of belonging. Without it, days can feel empty. This loss can lead to feelings of isolation or purposelessness. It's not uncommon to question your role in the world. These feelings can weigh heavily, affecting both mental and physical health. Recognizing these emotions is the first step in addressing them. It's important to understand that these feelings are normal and shared by many.

Building a new identity post-retirement is possible and necessary. Engaging in new hobbies can bring joy and a sense of accomplishment. Consider activities you've always wanted to try but have yet to have time for. Gardening, painting, or even joining a local club can open new avenues of interest. Volunteering is another way to find purpose. Helping others gives a sense of fulfilment and connects you with your community. Setting personal development goals also creates structure. These goals can be simple, like reading a new book each month, or more involved, like learning a new language. They give you a reason to get up each morning and a feeling of progress.

Sometimes, seeking professional help can make a big difference. Therapy or counselling provides a space to explore your feelings with guidance. If you notice signs of depression or anxiety, such as persistent sadness or a lack of interest in activities, consider reaching out for support. Local support groups for retirees also offer a place to share experiences and build connections. Talking with others who understand your situation can be comforting and insightful. These groups provide a platform to learn from others who have navigated similar transitions. They remind you that you're not alone in this experience.

To enhance emotional resilience, consider mindfulness and meditation practices. These activities help centre your thoughts and reduce stress. Start with simple breathing exercises. Focus on your breath for a few minutes each day. This practice helps clear your mind and brings a sense of calm. Meditation apps can guide you through more structured sessions if you want to explore further. These tools teach you to observe your thoughts without judgment. Over time, they build resilience, helping you manage emotions more effectively. Regular practice can improve your overall sense of well-being.

Exercise: Journaling for Reflection

Set aside time each day to write in a journal. Reflect on your feelings and thoughts. Ask yourself, "What did I enjoy today?" or "What am I looking forward to tomorrow?" This exercise helps you recognize patterns in your emotions and identify growth areas. It encourages gratitude, which boosts mood and satisfaction. Seeing your thoughts on paper can provide clarity and direction. Journaling is a private space for exploration and understanding.

As you navigate retirement, remember that change is part of life. It offers a chance to redefine who you are and what matters to you. You can build a rich and fulfilling life after work with the right strategies. This time is filled with opportunities to explore new passions and develop deeper connections. You can thrive in this new phase by embracing these changes and seeking support when needed.

8.3 ADDRESSING LONGEVITY RISK WITH CONFIDENCE

Longevity risk is the chance of living longer than your savings last. It's a genuine concern for many retirees. As life expectancy increases, so does the risk of outliving your money. This risk means you might need to fund more years of retirement than planned. Estimating how long you will live can feel tricky. But starting with a realistic picture of your life expectancy is important. Tools like online life expectancy calculators can help. These tools consider factors like your health, lifestyle, and family history. You can then adjust your financial plans to make sure your savings last as long as needed.

One way to reduce longevity risk is by delaying Social Security benefits. Waiting until you're older to start taking benefits increases your monthly payout. For instance, if you wait until age 70 instead of 62, you can get up to 30% more each month. This higher payout can make a big difference over time. It provides a steady, reliable income that can cover basic living expenses. This strategy is beneficial if you have other income sources and can afford to wait. It's a simple yet effective way to boost your financial security in later years.

Annuities can also help manage longevity risk. These financial products turn your savings into a guaranteed income for life. They provide peace of mind, knowing you won't outlive your money. Annuities come in different forms, letting you choose the one that fits your needs. Fixed annuities offer stable payouts, while variable annuities provide flexibility. They can be an excellent option to ensure a steady income stream. Adding an annuity to your retirement plan creates another layer of financial security. It's like having a safety net that supports you no matter how long you live.

Use tools that project your long-term financial needs to plan effectively for longevity. Retirement calculators and planning software can estimate how much money you'll need. They consider factors like inflation, future expenses, and expected income. Using these tools lets you see if your savings will last. It also helps identify any gaps. This can guide your decisions on how much more to save or invest. Regularly reviewing your projections keeps you informed and ready to adjust as needed. These tools empower you to take control of your financial future.

Consider the example of Sarah, a retiree who managed her longevity risk well. Sarah diversified her income sources. She had savings and a pension and decided to delay her Social Security benefits. This decision increased her monthly income significantly. She also purchased a small annuity. This annuity provided a guaranteed income that covered her essential expenses. By combining these strategies, Sarah ensured she had enough money to last her entire retirement. Her example shows how thoughtful planning and diversification can protect against longevity risk. It highlights the importance of using multiple income streams to maintain financial stability.

Addressing longevity risk involves understanding it and then taking steps to mitigate it. You can build a secure financial future by delaying Social Security, considering annuities, and using planning tools. These strategies provide the confidence that you will not outlive your savings. They offer peace of mind and help you enjoy retirement without financial stress.

8.4 STRATEGIES FOR A STRESS-FREE RETIREMENT TRANSITION

Social support plays a vital role in easing transitions. Family and community connections provide the support you need. They help you navigate the emotional and practical challenges of retirement.

Joining retirement groups can be beneficial. These groups offer a sense of community and belonging. They connect you with others who share similar experiences. This connection provides support and understanding. It helps reduce feelings of isolation. Engaging with the community also offers opportunities to stay active. Volunteering or taking part in local events keeps you involved. It can lead to new friendships and interests. This engagement enriches your retirement experience.

Consider the story of Mary, who transitioned smoothly into retirement. Mary planned a phased retirement. She gradually reduced her work hours over a year. This allowed her to slowly adapt to her new lifestyle. She used her extra time to explore hobbies like painting and gardening. Mary also joined a local retirement group. This group offered social activities and support. They helped her build a new social network. Mary found a balance between work and leisure. Her experience shows that with a bit of planning, retirement can be a fulfilling and enjoyable phase.

Planning a gradual transition, establishing a routine, and engaging with social support are essential. These steps help you adjust to your new lifestyle and reduce stress. They provide the tools you need to enjoy a fulfilling retirement. As you look forward to this new chapter, remember that it's an opportunity for growth and discovery. With the right approach, you can embrace retirement with confidence and optimism.

CHAPTER 9
FINAL EXERCISE AND REFLECTION

9.1 THE RETIREMENT READINESS CHECKLIST

At this point we would like you to revisit your Retirement Checklist once again.

Reflect on where you have gained knowledge and where you still want to learn more.

This process itself is illuminating. Congratulate yourself for coming this far.

Final Thoughts on your Retirement Ready Checklist

A readiness checklist can transform overwhelming feelings into clarity and confidence. This tool helps you assess how prepared you are for retirement. Think of it as a map highlighting what you need to focus on before retiring. Each item on the checklist represents a key area of your life that deserves attention. You gain insight into your current state and what you need to address by ticking off items. It ensures you cover all aspects of your life, from finances to health, making your transition smoother.

Start by examining your financial security. Ask yourself if you have enough savings to support your desired lifestyle. Consider your income sources, like pensions and Social Security. Assess if they align with your spending needs. Look at your debts and create a plan to manage or eliminate them. Make sure you have an emergency fund for unexpected expenses. This financial assessment forms the backbone of your checklist. It provides a clear picture of your financial health and guides your planning. Knowing where you stand financially allows you to make informed decisions about spending and saving in retirement.

Next, evaluate your health and wellness. Consider your current health status and any ongoing medical needs. Do you have a plan for healthcare coverage, such as Medicare or private insurance? Think about your lifestyle choices and how they impact your well-being. Include regular check-ups and preventive care in your plan. This part of the checklist ensures you prioritize your health, which is crucial for enjoying retirement. Staying healthy allows you to remain active and engaged in activities you love. It also helps prevent medical costs from eating into your savings.

Social and emotional readiness is another critical area. Reflect on your social network and support system. Are you maintaining relationships with friends and family? Consider how you will stay connected and involved in your community. Plan activities that keep you socially active and emotionally fulfilled. This could include volunteer work, joining clubs, or pursuing hobbies. Preparing for these aspects ensures you have a balanced and fulfilling retirement. It prevents feelings of isolation and helps you find purpose and joy in your daily life.

Using the checklist to identify gaps is like highlighting areas that need attention. Compare your current situation with your desired retirement vision. Are there discrepancies between the two? This comparison helps you spot weaknesses in your plan. Once you've identified these gaps, consider what actions you need to take. Set specific goals to address them. For example, if your savings fall short, explore ways to increase your income or reduce expenses. If your health plan is lacking, research additional coverage options. Addressing these gaps strengthens your readiness and boosts your confidence.

Some gaps may require professional advice. Feel free to seek help for complex issues. Financial advisors can offer insights into optimizing your investments and savings. Healthcare professionals can guide you in managing medical needs. Counsellors or therapists can provide support for emotional challenges. Engaging with experts ensures you receive tailored advice that fits your unique circumstances. This support can make a significant difference in your planning process. It provides reassurance and clarity, helping you make the best decisions for your future.

A well-crafted readiness checklist is more than just a to-do list. It's a comprehensive tool that empowers you to take control of your retirement. You can enter retirement with peace of mind and enthusiasm by systematically assessing each area of your life. This checklist acts as a guide, leading you toward a secure and satisfying retirement. It keeps you focused and organized, ensuring nothing is overlooked. As you work through each item, you lay the groundwork for a fulfilling and enjoyable life after work.

EMBRACING A FULFILLING RETIREMENT

"Your legacy is every life you have touched."

MAYA ANGELOU

For many retirees, this newfound freedom opens doors to explore the world in ways never before possible. Travel offers more than just a change of scenery. It allows you to see the world from new angles, meet people from different walks of life, and dive into diverse cultures. Whether strolling through the historic streets of Italy or exploring the serene landscapes of Arizona, travel can enrich your life in countless ways.

Exploring new places can broaden your horizons and offer fresh perspectives. Each destination presents unique stories and traditions. You might walk through ancient ruins in Greece, feeling the weight of history beneath your feet. Or you'll find yourself in a bustling market in Mexico, where vibrant colours and lively sounds fill the air. These experiences deepen your understanding of the world and yourself. They encourage you to think differently and embrace change. As you immerse yourself in new environments, you learn to appreciate the beauty and diversity of life.

Travel also presents opportunities for personal growth and learning. Every trip can teach you something new- a language, a recipe, or a craft. Engaging with locals allows you to see life through their eyes. You might discover simple joys, like a quiet sunset on a beach in the Bahamas or the rich flavours of a French café. Travelling encourages curiosity and adaptability. It challenges you to step out of your comfort zone and try new things. This spirit of adventure can lead to personal transformation and renewed zest for life.

Planning your travel experiences to fit your lifestyle ensures that each journey is enjoyable and stress-free. Consider destinations that align with your interests and health needs. If you love nature, national parks like those in California offer breathtaking views and outdoor activities. For those passionate about history, places like The Alamo in Texas provide rich narratives and cultural insights. Balance adventure with relaxation to avoid burnout. After a day of exploring, allow time to unwind with a good book or a leisurely walk. This balance keeps your travels fulfilling without overwhelming your senses.

Budget-friendly travel options make exploring more accessible. Many airlines and hotels offer senior discounts. Using travel rewards programs can reduce costs significantly. Booking flights on off-peak days, like Tuesdays or Wednesdays, can save money. Travelling during the off-season cuts expenses and lets you enjoy attractions without the crowds. Consider accommodations with kitchens. Preparing your meals can cut down on dining costs. Public transportation provides a cost-effective way to explore cities and meet locals. These strategies help you travel smartly, ensuring your adventures are affordable and memorable.

Inspiring stories from fellow retirees can ignite your wanderlust and offer practical insights.

Leaving a Legacy: Impacting Future Generations

As you enter retirement, the notion of legacy often becomes more prominent. A legacy is more than just money or property. It's about the mark you leave on the world. It reflects your values, the lessons you've learned, and the traditions you cherish. It's about contributing to the community and fostering progress. Consider how your actions can inspire others and drive change when you think about your legacy. Whether it's through volunteering, mentoring, or advocating for causes you believe in, your influence can ripple through time, impacting not only your immediate surroundings but also society at large.

Leaving a legacy means instilling values and traditions in future generations. It's about passing down the wisdom and practices that have shaped your life. You can start by sharing family stories and recounting tales of perseverance, love, and courage. These narratives carry lessons that transcend time, teaching younger generations about resilience and empathy. Family gatherings provide opportunities to reinforce these values. As you share meals and celebrate traditions, you strengthen the bonds that connect your family. These moments are the threads that weave the fabric of your legacy, creating a tapestry that reflects your life's essence.

Creating impactful legacy projects can leave a lasting impression. Consider establishing scholarships or educational programs that open doors for aspiring students. Investing in education empowers individuals to pursue their dreams and contribute to their communities. Documenting your family history and stories ensures your legacy is preserved for years. Compile a collection of photographs, letters, and anecdotes that vividly depict your family's journey. This record becomes a treasure trove of memories, offering future generations a glimpse into their roots and heritage.

Involving your family in legacy-building fosters unity and collaboration. Please encourage them to participate in projects that reflect shared values and interests. Establishing a family foundation or charitable trust allows you to support causes you care about collectively. These initiatives provide a platform for family members to engage in meaningful work together, strengthening bonds and creating a sense of purpose. Organizing annual family traditions and gatherings reinforces connections and creates a sense of belonging. Whether it's a holiday celebration or a summer reunion, these events become cherished occasions that bring everyone closer.

Consider the story of a retiree who founded a community library. This individual recognized a need for accessible resources and took action to make a difference. The library became a hub for learning and connection, serving as a testament to the retiree's commitment to education and community. Their legacy lives on in the lives touched by the library's offerings, from children discovering the joy of reading to adults pursuing lifelong learning. This example illustrates how a single initiative can create a lasting impact, shaping the community and enriching lives.

Another retiree chose to pass down artisanal skills through family workshops. They gathered children and grandchildren to share the art of woodworking, weaving, or painting. These workshops became opportunities for skill-building and storytelling as techniques and traditions were passed from generation to generation. The retiree's legacy became a tapestry of creativity and craftsmanship, woven with the threads of shared experiences and cherished memories. These skills, once honed, become gifts that future generations can carry forward, ensuring that the legacy of artistry and craftsmanship endures.

Even small actions can contribute to a meaningful legacy. Planting a garden that blooms each spring, volunteering at a local shelter, or supporting a neighborhood project can all leave a mark. These gestures demonstrate a commitment to nurturing and improving the world around you. They show that a legacy isn't always about grand gestures. It's about the consistency of small acts of kindness and the values they represent. These actions inspire others to follow suit, creating a ripple effect far beyond their initial impact.

Legacy-building involves a blend of reflection, action, and collaboration. It requires you to consider what matters most and how to make a difference. It calls for the courage to take steps that align with your values and create positive change. Engaging your family and community amplifies your efforts and ensures that your legacy extends beyond your lifetime. As you navigate this path, remember that your legacy reflects who you are and what you stand for. It is a testament to the choices you've made and the values you've embraced.

This exploration of legacy invites you to think about the broader impact of your actions. It encourages you to reflect on what you wish to leave behind. As you continue to shape your legacy, consider how you can contribute to the greater good. Whether through education, community involvement, or family traditions, your legacy is a tapestry woven with intention and care. It is a gift that future generations will cherish and build upon, carrying your influence into a brighter future.

As you conclude this chapter, remember that your legacy is a living testament to your life's journey. It reflects the values you've held dear and your impact on the world. As you look ahead, embrace the opportunity to create a legacy that resonates with your heart and inspires those who follow. Your legacy is a beacon of hope and possibility, guiding future generations toward a path of kindness, wisdom, and compassion.

Are you Retirement Ready?

As we conclude our exploration of retirement planning, we find ourselves at a pivotal moment in history. The landscape before us is complex and challenging, shaped by five fundamental forces that demand our attention and action. We've witnessed how increased longevity; a triumph of modern medicine, has introduced new complexities and exposed societal inequities that cannot be ignored.

The transition from defined benefit to defined contribution plans represents not just a shift in financial mechanisms, but a fundamental reimagining of retirement security for millions of people. Perhaps most pressing is the persistent challenge of converting retirement savings into sustainable lifetime income – a puzzle that continues to challenge even the most sophisticated financial minds.

The stark reality of the access divide, leaving 57 million Americans without employer-sponsored retirement plans, combined with troubling racial and ethnic disparities in retirement savings, underscores the urgent need for systemic change. These challenges have been further amplified by recent global disruptions, including the COVID-19 pandemic, market volatility, and inflation, which have shaken retirement confidence to its core. Yet within these challenges lie opportunities for innovation, reform, and progress.

When we look to the future, our task is clear: we must work collectively – as individuals, institutions, and as a society – to build a retirement system that is not only robust and sustainable but also equitable and inclusive. The road ahead may be demanding, but the stakes are too high and the consequences too significant to do anything less than rise to meet this historic challenge.

As we draw our exploration to a close, it's worth reflecting on the deeply personal journey that retirement planning represents. Throughout these pages, we've transformed complex financial concepts into actionable steps, each designed to empower you in crafting your unique retirement story. From the foundational elements of creating a retirement vision to the nuanced strategies of tax-efficient withdrawals, from healthcare planning to emotional well-being, we've woven together a comprehensive tapestry of retirement wisdom.

The heart of this journey lies not just in the accumulation of knowledge, but in its practical application to create a retirement that truly resonates with your values and aspirations.

You now stand equipped with tools that extend far beyond mere financial planning – you have a holistic framework that encompasses your emotional, social, and financial well-being. This integrated approach recognizes that true retirement success lies in the harmonious balance of all these elements. The exercises, strategies, and real-world examples provided throughout this book serve as your compass, guiding you toward a retirement that is not only secure but deeply fulfilling.

As you step forward into this new chapter, remember that retirement planning is a dynamic journey, not a static destination.

Your path will evolve, requiring flexibility and occasional course corrections.

Embrace these changes with confidence, knowing you possess the knowledge to adapt and thrive.

Connect with others on similar journeys, seek guidance when needed, and most importantly, remain excited about the possibilities that lie ahead. Your retirement years represent an unprecedented opportunity to rewrite your story, pursue long-held dreams, and create a legacy that truly matters.

The future beckons with promise, and you are now Retirement Ready - Prepared to embark on the next phase of your life with intention, assurance, and purpose.

KEEPING THE FUTURE SECURE

Now that you have everything you need to create your retirement blueprint, it's time to pass on your knowledge and show other readers where they can find the guidance they're looking for.

Simply by leaving your honest opinion of this book on Amazon, you'll help other soon-to-be retirees find clear, practical information about securing their financial future. In a world where retirement planning feels increasingly complex, your review can be the beacon that guides others to the answers they need.

Thank you for your help. Financial wisdom grows stronger when we share it with others – and you're helping me ensure that everyone has access to the retirement planning guidance they deserve; no matter where they are starting.

Click here to leave your review on Amazon

REFERENCES

American Association of Retired Persons. (n.d.). A step-by-step guide to Medicare enrollment. Retrieved from https://www.aarp.org/health/medicare-insurance/enrollment-guide/

Bankrate. (n.d.). 5 popular annuities for retirees. Retrieved from https://www.bankrate.com/retirement/popular-annuities-for-retirees/

Citi Life and Money. (n.d.). Vision boards for retirement planning. Retrieved from https://www.lifeandmoney.citi.com/lam/articles/milestones/retirement/vision-board-retirement

Crews Bank. (n.d.). Securing your legacy: The importance of wills and trusts. Retrieved from https://www.crews.bank/blog/securing-your-legacy-the-importance-of-wills-and-trusts

Fidelity Investments. (n.d.). Six tips to help reduce estate taxes. Retrieved from https://www.fidelity.com/learning-center/personal-finance/how-to-avoid-estate-taxes

Fidelity Investments. (n.d.). Tax-savvy withdrawals in retirement. Retrieved from https://www.fidelity.com/viewpoints/retirement/tax-savvy-withdrawals

Fisher Investments. (n.d.). Retirement in the U.S.: A history to today. Retrieved from https://www.fisherinvestments.com/en-us/insights/business-401k/retiring-in-the-us-brief-history

Forbes Advisor. (2024). Best long-term care insurance companies of 2024. Retrieved from https://www.forbes.com/advisor/life-insurance/best-long-term-care-insurance/

Forbes Health. (n.d.). 11 meaningful ways older adults can volunteer right now. Retrieved from https://www.forbes.com/health/healthy-aging/volunteer-opportunities-for-older-adults/

Forbes Health. (n.d.). Aging in place remodeling: A checklist for senior homes. Retrieved from https://www.forbes.com/health/healthy-aging/aging-in-place-remodeling/

Fulton Bank. (n.d.). Five expenses to consider before relocating for retirement. Retrieved from https://www.fultonbank.com/Education-Center/Retirement/5-expenses-to-consider-before-relocating-for-retirement

Gudeman Law. (2024). How to handle complex family dynamics in estate planning. Retrieved from https://www.gudemanlaw.com/2024/06/24/how-to-handle-complex-family-dynamics-in-estate-planning/

HelpGuide. (n.d.). Adjusting to retirement: Handling depression and stress. Retrieved from https://www.helpguide.org/aging/healthy-aging/adjusting-to-retirement

HSA Central. (n.d.). The tax benefits of a health savings account. Retrieved from https://www.hsacentral.net/consumers/tax-benefits-health-savings-account/

Internal Revenue Service. (n.d.). Retirement plan and IRA required minimum distributions FAQs. Retrieved from https://www.irs.gov/retirement-plans/retirement-plan-and-ira-required-minimum-distributions-faqs

Investopedia. (n.d.). 9 ways to boost your Social Security benefits. Retrieved from https://www.investopedia.com/articles/retirement/112116/10-social-security-secrets-could-boost-your-benefits.asp

JP Morgan Asset Management. (2024). Guide to retirement planning. Retrieved from am.jpmorgan.com

Mayo Clinic. (n.d.). A surprising key to healthy aging: Strong social connections. Retrieved from https://mcpress.mayoclinic.org/healthy-aging/a-surprising-key-to-healthy-aging-strong-social-connections/

Morningstar. (n.d.). A retirement readiness checklist. Retrieved from https://www.morningstar.com/personal-finance/retirement-readiness-checklist

My Farewelling. (n.d.). Creating a legacy project for a loved one. Retrieved from https://www.myfarewelling.com/article/creating-a-legacy-project-for-a-loved-one

National Academies of Sciences, Engineering, and Medicine. (n.d.). Economic impact of family caregiving. Retrieved from https://www.ncbi.nlm.nih.gov/books/NBK396402/

Osher Foundation. (n.d.). Osher Lifelong Learning Institutes. Retrieved from https://www.osherfoundation.org/olli.html

Quadra Wealth. (n.d.). How holistic retirement planning can transform your life. Retrieved from https://quadrawealth.com/articles/power-of-holistic-retirement-planning/

Retire Better Now. (2023). The 10 best 55+ communities in the United States [2023]. Retrieved from https://www.retirebetternow.com/blog/best-55-communities-in-the-united-states/

Schwab. (n.d.). Dealing with market volatility in retirement. Retrieved from https://www.schwab.com/learn/story/market-volatility-retirement-what-if-you-havent-prepared

Smart Asset. (n.d.). How mutual funds can be used for retirement. Retrieved from https://smartasset.com/retirement/mutual-funds-retirement

Social Security Administration. (n.d.). The changing impact of Social Security on retirement income. Retrieved from https://www.ssa.gov/policy/docs/ssb/v65n3/v65n3p1.html

U.S. News & Money. (n.d.). 14 top travel destinations for retirees. Retrieved from https://money.usnews.com/money/retirement/baby-boomers/articles/top-travel-destinations-for-retirees

U.S. News & Money. (2019, April 3). 6 retirees share their second-career stories. Retrieved from https://money.usnews.com/money/retirement/second-careers/articles/2019-04-03/6-retirees-share-their-second-career-stories

University of Washington. (n.d.). The retirement process: A psychological and emotional journey. Retrieved from https://retirees.uw.edu/resources/retirement-transitions/the-retirement-process-a-psychological-and-emotional-journey/

Vestwell. (2023). 2023 retirement trends report. Retrieved from https://www.vestwell.com/read/2023-retirement-trends-report

Wealth Enhancement. (n.d.). Values-based retirement planning for women. Retrieved from https://www.wealthenhancement.com/s/blog/values-based-retirement-planning-for-women-simple-powerful-strategies-MCEWAUI5WHIBD7XBCTBXVBTJVT2Q

Where You Live Matters. (n.d.). Managing the emotions of downsizing. Retrieved from https://www.whereyoulivematters.org/resources/dealing-with-downsizing-emotions/

www.ingramcontent.com/pod-product-compliance
Lightning Source LLC
LaVergne TN
LVHW100322210926
848480LV00003B/1226
9798230749554